MY LIFE WITH
SNOOPY

MY LIFE WITH
SNOOPY

How One Shelter Dog's Love
Changed a Man's Life and
Other *Tails* of Adventure

JOEY CAMEN

Opulent Press
5850 W 3rd St., #332
Los Angeles, CA 90036
Email: joey@voicecomic.com

Published 2014 by Opulent Press

Printed in the United States of America

17 16 15 14   2 3 4 5

ISBN: 978-0-9903423-0-4

Library of Congress Control Number: 2013947404

Back cover photo by Robert James of Paradise Photography.
Front cover photo by Joey Camen.

This book is dedicated to all pet owners
who have loved and lost their best friend.
May my stories give you a good laugh and a needed cry.

CONTENTS

TO THE READER

Dear Reader:

Thank you for buying my book. The following pages are the story of a man and his dog...me and my dog...my dog, Snoopy. It's my journey...my time with man's best friend. Snoopy was, without a doubt, my best friend. His imprint upon my heart and mind are forever with me.

I work in the entertainment industry as a professional voice actor, standup comedian, actor, and writer. I'm not a household name. I'm known mostly within the community I work, rather than to the general public. However, you may or maybe you don't know, some of the projects I've worked on over the years.

Some early voiceover performances include, the original voice of Natural Smurf for the *Smurfs* cartoon series...being a designated voice for McGruff the Crime Dog...the voice of Monstar Bang in the movie *Space Jam*, and more recently, providing voices for video games; *Transformers: Dark of the Moon*...*Mafia II*...the *Sam and Max* online game, and the hugely popular *Skylanders* series for children, as the voices of Terrafin and Boomer. If you'd like to see more of my credits, you can go to the International Movie Database www.imdb.com, and type in my name. Or you can visit my voiceover website at www.voicecomic.com and listen to some of my voices.

I started working in show business as a standup

comedian while still a teenager, just seventeen years-old and a bit of an introvert, except when I was performing on stage, which may seem like an oxymoron. Many performers are shy off-stage and in their personal lives. The stage, the spotlight, the microphone, the craft of acting, the camera; any one of them can make a performer come alive.

Less than a year into working on my standup act, at the ripe old age of eighteen, I was introduced to legendary voice over actor and teacher, Daws Butler, better known as the voices of Yogi Bear, Huckleberry Hound, Cap'n Crunch and many others. Daws saw a bit of himself in me. He was also a standup comedian in his late teens and from the Midwest. He took me under his wing as his protégé. The master of voice gave this insecure kid from Detroit a new confidence, and taught him to improve his vocal characterizations and acting skills.

In my early standup comedy days at the Comedy Store comedy club in Hollywood, I shared the stage with performers like Richard Pryor, whose short-lived 1977 TV series; The Richard Pryor Show, I was cast as a bit player, and got to perform in a few sketches with Richard. I was twenty. I was also one of the few standup comedians whom Richard allowed to go on before him to warm up the crowd when he worked out material for his comedy albums. Classics like, "Is it Something I Said?" and "Wanted: Richard Pryor - Live in Concert."

Other performers I worked with are Robin Williams, Jim Carrey, David Letterman, Jay Leno, Rosanne Barr, and more. And I more than held my own. In the past I've acted in sitcoms...performed standup comedy in colleges... written and performed one person shows...was an opening act for rock and roll bands and singers like the late Marvin

Gaye...performed in main showrooms in Las Vegas and headlined in comedy clubs throughout the United States.

My standup act was pretty out there, doing voices and characters that even today would be considered wild or risqué. More in the vein of my boyhood idol, Jonathan Winters, than a comedian telling jokes with set-ups and punch lines. I just never became as famous as many of those I've worked with. It doesn't make me any less talented, funny, or entertaining. It happens in every line of work. I've always been a very private person, but I want *you, Dear Reader,* to know about my background, the person who wrote this book, the person who's sharing his story.

The story of me and my dog Snoopy has brought me out of my private shell to share with you the good, the fun, and the tragic times we had together. I was forty when he came into my life. The phrase "Life Begins at Forty" took on special meaning. Our time together changed me for the better...and he continues to influence me. This dog memoir you hold in your hands as a book, or on your Kindle, or other device, is my love letter to my dog. Though I've written many screenplays, comedy routines, and monologues over the years; *My Life with Snoopy: How One Shelter Dog's Love Changed a Man's Life and Other Tails of Adventure* is my book-writing debut.

I hope my stories inspire you to get your own shelter dog and let a special kind of love into your life. May it teach you what I've learned; that anyone, no matter how hurt or wounded in life, can find love on four feet, and carry that love into relationships with two feet. Enjoy!

Joey Camen —Author

ACKNOWLEDGEMENTS

Whether good, bad or indifferent; I would like to thank all the memorable pets, people, and circumstances which came through my and Snoopy's lives and are mentioned in the following pages.

I'd especially like to thank Wendy, my wife and partner, for being Snoopy's mom. She took care of him alongside me for many years. He was as much her child as he was mine. Her caring and loving presence, particularly during the hard times, made life more pleasant and I am grateful.

I also want to thank my editors: Alexandra Kogan of Buena Editing Services for her intuitiveness and literary skills, and Juliet Nordeen of ArtChi's Voice Publishing for her writing expertise and wisdom in the dog world. Their care and suggestions were extremely valuable in making my stories "pop" for the reader...My friend, Barrie Schwortz, for his help in enhancing the photos throughout the book... Robert James of Paradise Photography for his amazing *family photo* on the back cover...Sheila Cowley of Creative Fuel Studios for her hard work and awesome design of the book cover.

The PublishNext team: Randy Kuckuck, the boss man, for his insight and oversight...Senior Editor Trey Schorr for his helpful suggestions...Kiran Spees for her excellent

InDesign skills, and Trudy Catterfeld not only for her vast knowledge in marketing, but for her kind heart and going *way beyond* the extra mile in making this book the best it could be.

And most importantly...this book would not have been possible without my beloved dog, Snoopy, who opened my heart to a love I could have never imagined. Though our road was sometimes difficult, he gave me strength to write about our adventures. I believe our stories are universal...in a universe where people love dogs. I celebrate his beautiful life the best I know how—with words. This is for you, my boy. I love you.

INTRODUCTION

Most pet owners, and especially dog owners, like to think their pets are special. I am one of them. My dog Snoopy was truly special. He was a one-of-a-kind Sheltie-mix, most likely with American Eskimo—two smart breeds. He looked like he was half and half, but I never really knew for certain. In the looks department, he was the Brad Pitt, the Johnny Depp, the George Clooney of dogs. A very handsome boy. Or for older folks, he was the Kirk Douglas, Cary Grant, the Errol Flynn of dogs.

Everyone thinks their dog or doggies are physically beautiful, even people who own a Mexican hairless, or a Chinese crested. For thirteen-plus years, whoever saw my dog for the first time, some of the first words out of their mouths were comments like, "What a pretty dog," "That's a good-looking animal," or "Handsome." He was. Even the vet who euthanized him commented on his good looks.

Snoopy's disposition was sweet, sweet, sweet. He had a unique affect on people, even those who never met him. For example: a friend of mine, who adored Snoopy, asked for a picture of him to give to her ten year old daughter. The kid instantly fell in love with his photo and kept it on her wall in her bedroom for several years. When she was told of his passing, she broke down crying as if she had known him. He was one-in-a-million.

We were together thirteen years, two months, and four days. But who's counting? I am. When you have a love like this, every day is worth counting. Not that I counted every day he was alive, though I always remembered the anniversary of his adoption, September 9th, 1997. A life-changing day for us both. If you've ever adopted an animal into your life and home, fallen in love and then lost them, you know how I feel.

Life is short, and it's even shorter for our pet friends. My deep connection with Snoopy has to do with my childhood. All I will say now is that he helped heal a 30 year-old wound that no therapy or counseling ever could have. I am eternally grateful for having him in my life. I miss him so much it hurts, I don't know when or if the hurt will entirely go away, and I may not want it to.

In the end, he was in so much pain; he was getting worse day by day. The last thing I wanted to do was put him down. It was and still is, unthinkable to me. If he could have outlived me, I would have been very happy. But that's not the way it is for these wonderful creatures that come into our lives.

If there is some *thing* called heaven it would be for our four-legged friends. Snoopy *was* an angel and he's gone to wherever he's gone to, and he's no longer in pain. The good thing about God is that backwards it spells "dog."

Boy, do I, and did I, love my dog.

-1-

ANIMALS IN MY EARLY YEARS

I came into the world in 1957. Birthplace: My mother's womb...Detroit, Michigan...the Motor City...Motown. I was a street kid, a city kid, with an aversion to the more upscale suburbs. Being told they were filled with snotty rich kids, who wanted to be around them?

The neighborhood I grew up in...well, I've never really grown up. I'll begin again. The neighborhood I *first lived in* as a kid was on a street called Ward, on the east side of town, one block shy of Eight Mile Road, between Schaefer Highway and Meyers Road. Me and my family lived in a small red brick house, less than 800 square feet, built in 1944. It was lower-middle class. Some might have considered it a rough neighborhood, but it was all I knew. The ethnicity of the residents on the surrounding streets, which became my world for the first nine years of my life, were primarily Blacks, then Jews, Italians, Polish, and a bit of White Trash. I didn't know anyone in my neighborhood who had pets back then.

My father was an eleventh-grade, high school dropout. He worked as a "commission only" upholstery salesman—a gruff, blue-collar guy, who wore cheap polyester suits and had no clue how bad they looked. His job required him to drive a step van into some of the worst neighborhoods in America at the time, and show potential customers samples of fabric that their ratty couches and chairs could be reupholstered with—on credit. If he got the sale, he'd have to carry—or drag rather—the couch or chairs out of their home by *himself,* and load it into the step van. Then he'd get the heck out of there before he got robbed.

My mother, a sweet, plump woman with kind eyes and unfulfilled dreams of becoming a school teacher, worked part-time in a bindery, on an assembly line, gluing together pads of paper, books, magazines and whatever else they threw her way. I can't imagine the chemicals she had to breathe in back in those days. This was in addition to having four children by 1961.

Our house was animal-less. Although, I did have a teddy bear when I was three. Aunt Esther, my mother's sister, a heavyset woman with bad grammar and matching breath, owned a dog named Bushy that I loved. Bushy was a large reddish-brown mix. Possibly a Lab with a bit of Irish Setter, I'm not sure. He was a big friendly boy. When we'd visited I was allowed to walk Bushy around the neighborhood. One of my fondest boyhood memories is of walking him in the winter with several inches of snow and ice on the ground. I was about five or six. Bushy would pull me as I hung onto his leash and slid along the ice-covered sidewalk. I'd pretend I was dog sledding—I laughed and kept falling down on the ice over and over again, each time getting back up as Bushy barked, and took me on another wild ride down the block.

I was a small boy and it took all my strength to keep him under control. It was great fun. I absolutely loved it.

At eight I acquired my first pet, or pets. Snails. Yes, snails. Slimy little brown creatures that lived tucked inside their shells. I dug them out of a shallow pond next to an industrial building across Eight Mile Road. I put a few dozen in an old aluminum pot that I got from my mother, covered them with water and kept them in our basement. I thought they were cool-looking, except they didn't smell very good. The longer I kept them, the worse their smell became—it was bad. I really didn't know what I was doing, or how they survived. The smell upsetting my parents made me want to keep them even more. After several arguments with my mother I talked her into buying me goldfish in exchange for me getting rid of the snails. Back to the pond they went.

She bought me two goldfish, fish food, and a half-gallon oval-shaped fish bowl with a round opening on top about the size of a large mayonnaise jar. It was enough room for a couple of goldfish to swim around in comfortably. I can't remember the exact details, but my goldfish lived only a few weeks and then suddenly they were floating on top of the water—dead. I didn't cry or throw a fit or anything. At eight years old I didn't have any emotional attachment to a couple of fish that could fit on an order of salmon sushi. Down the toilet they went. It was the end of my time with the fishes, or any other pets...for a while.

-2-

TUCSON, ARIZONA, THE NEW SCHOOL, AND BUBBIE SARAH

The year was 1966. I was nine years old. One day, out of nowhere, my father announced, "We're moving to Tucson, Arizona." Goodbye Detroit. Goodbye school. Goodbye friends. Hello, Tucson. My father had received a job offer from his older brother, my Uncle Harry, who had moved to Tucson years earlier. Uncle Harry was a balding man with a fake smile and dark leathery skin from doing construction work in the Arizona sun. I don't remember what kind of job my father accepted, but he obviously thought it was better than selling upholstery recovering to cash-strapped families.

I did not like Tucson. Going from living in a multi-ethic neighborhood in Detroit, to living among lily-white people with tans—who had rocks instead of grass on their lawns—was mind-boggling. Plus, it was miserably hot outside. Walking to school in 100-degree heat and watching it literally rise off the pavement sucked big-time.

During this time I saw my first lizard. Actually, it was a

baby lizard. It was pretty cool. I was sitting in math class. The boy seated in the desk next to me, wearing a tank top, shorts, and sandals—which was a far cry from how kids dressed in Detroit—was playing with a baby lizard he kept in his pants pocket. It was greenish-brown, scaly, no more than four-inches long and very fast. He would hold it in his hand down around his stomach and then let it go. The baby lizard would quickly run across his chest and he'd grab it before it got to his shoulder or neck, and he'd do it over-and-over again. I'd never seen anything like it.

The image of him playing with a baby lizard in math class has always stayed with me. He probably would have thought it equally odd if he'd had to live in Detroit in the winter after living in the desert his whole life, walking to school in the freezing cold, wearing a padded jacket, and getting hit in the face with a snowball thrown by a black kid.

My biggest worry in Tucson wasn't adapting to the heat or not having any friends. It was the school curriculum. Everything from Math to English to Physical Education was much harder than what I had been taught in the Detroit Public School system. I did okay, but I had to study twice as hard to pass the tests.

My parents didn't let me do much outside school, except go to the local Jewish Community Center where I learned how to swim in an Olympic-sized swimming pool. I learned the breaststroke, how to hold my breath underwater for a minute or so, float on my back, all kinds of fun aquatic stuff. I can still smell the pungent odor of the pool's chlorine and the chemical stink of Coppertone suntan lotion on my skin. I didn't care for either smell. I did get a tan. I liked how it made me look. It made me feel like another person. I had a few cousins, my Uncle Harry's kids, who were several years older than me and rarely around. I didn't like my older brother, my older sister was mentally disturbed, and my other brother was four years younger. I couldn't really hang-out with a five year-old for too long.

I became sort of loner in Arizona. Plus, my Uncle Harry and his wife, my Aunt Reva—a loud, whiny woman, who wore big-framed sunglasses even while indoors—were not the friendliest people. Aunt Reva once called me and my siblings "a bunch of animals" because we were screaming and running around her house, like kids do. This seriously upset my mother. With all I've been through in my life, I now take being called an *animal* a compliment.

Tucson didn't last very long. Maybe four months. Time seems to move slower when you're a kid. Mom didn't like Tucson or Aunt Reva. Dad obviously didn't like it either, because he quit his job. I think mom might have had something to do with it. We were soon on our way back to Detroit and living in a rougher neighborhood than our last one.

All six of us—Mom, Dad, me, my two brothers and sister—moved into a cramped two-bedroom apartment with my grandma Sarah, my father's mother. Us kids called her Bubbie Sarah. "Bubbie" means grandmother in Yiddish. Bubbie Sarah was a kick-ass Russian immigrant and a little nutty. She had a thick Russian accent, wore old lady orthopedic shoes and pantyhose thick as a tee-shirt. She spoke her mind and took no crap from anyone. Dad was flat broke, but he got his job back selling upholstery. We were going to have to wait until he saved enough money to get us a new place. Bubbie Sarah's neighborhood was considered, for lack of better words, "very crime ridden."

It was a scary neighborhood. You could get robbed going to the grocery store a block away. I remember walking with Bubbie Sarah along Dexter Avenue, which was about fifty yards from her apartment, when a black boy around my age sneaked up behind us and tried to snatch her purse. He didn't get it. Bubbie Sarah held it tight, yelled some Yiddish swear-words at him, which probably sounded like Martian to the kid, and he took off running. It sounded like Martian to me, too.

We lived with Bubbie Sarah in her cramped apartment for about two months in late summer, before the new school year. I didn't mind. I was her favorite grandkid. I was named after her late husband, my grandpa Joseph, who *died the day I was born.* His tombstone has my name engraved on it, or both our names rather, and my date of birth is listed as his date of death. These were rather odd circumstances, but it didn't bother me. I found it more fascinating than morbid.

Bubbie Sarah treated me special, like I was his reincarnation or something. She called me "Yosala," which means Joey in Yiddish. Whatever food she made, I got first, and she was a great cook. Everything was made from scratch. I got the biggest pieces of her homemade lemon meringue pie, kreplach (which is more or less Jewish ravioli), gefilte fish, and homemade pickled green tomatoes and cucumbers which she canned and kept under the kitchen sink.

Bubbie Sarah didn't care too much for my older siblings, which was odd for a grandmother. She'd call them uncomplimentary names in Yiddish, making fun of my sister, who was fat, and my brother, who had severely bucked-teeth. This didn't sit well with my mother, who

Bubbie Sarah also didn't like, and ordered around like her personal slave. My father would barely speak up to defend his wife or children; he was scared of his mother. All this made for an interesting dynamic, to say the least. I had fun though, but everyone else wasn't too happy. I loved my Bubbie Sarah.

About a year after our stay, Bubbie Sarah's neighborhood was the focal point of Detroit's infamous 1967 summer riot. The shops along Dexter Avenue were looted and burned to the ground. I have one memory of visiting her during that time. I sat on the windowsill of her apartment window on the eighth floor and watched the action on Dexter below. There were several black kids, around my age and younger, going into stores and running out with groceries and other items as their mothers frantically yelled at them to hurry up. Detroit was in major turmoil back then.

After living with Bubbie Sarah we moved to a slightly better neighborhood. My parents rented the bottom floor of a two-story A-frame brick house with a big backyard that was sectioned off as two separate housing units. I was almost ten years-old. The time I spent in this new home, roughly a year and a half, were some of the most memorable and tragic times of my life.

The new house was further east than our previous home, before the move to Tucson. The street we lived on was called Roselawn. It was in-between Curtis Avenue and Six Mile Road, a.k.a., McNichols Road. It was primarily a black neighborhood, with us being one of the few white families. Many of my memories are vivid for that year—1967.

I was the only white kid in my fifth-grade English class. I was small and looked young for my age. Most people thought I was around six years-old. It didn't bother me; it was just the way it was. I made several new friends and had a great time in school. I was even a Safety Patrol boy. One thing that I thought was very cool about our new neighborhood at the time; Stevie Wonder, the legendary Motown singer, had lived one street over and a couple blocks down on Greenlawn Street. Greenlawn...Roselawn. Whoever named those streets must have liked lawns. Stevie had already left home, but his family was still there. His younger brother attended the same school as me, John J. Bagley Elementary.

-3-

MY FIRST SNOOPY

Spring of 1967. One Sunday afternoon my Uncle Moshe, who was married to my Aunt Esther, came to visit. Uncle Moshe seemed like a quiet man, the polar opposite of his wife. He was tall...well, everyone was tall to me back then, and he sported a brown mustache and wire-rimmed glasses. To my surprise, he had brought a puppy with him. A purebred Labrador Retriever only a couple of months old. He was sort of a chocolate brown...so small and so, so cute. The odd thing about this...the puppy was for *me*. Not my parents...not my brothers or sister...*me*. He gave the puppy to *me*.

My parents told me I could keep him as long as I agreed to take care of him and clean up after him. No problem. I was a very responsible ten year-old. Another odd thing about this; I didn't know my Uncle Moshe very well, he had rarely ever spoken to me. He was a mailman and someone gave him the puppy, and he chose to give the pup to me. Maybe he had realized how much I enjoyed his dog, Bushy. Whatever the reason, Moshe was now the coolest, most incredible uncle on the planet. Uncle Moshe was forever in my heart.

I named my new puppy Snoopy, after the Charles Schultz *Peanuts* character. I didn't care that he wasn't a Beagle. I don't remember having ever seen a real Beagle back then. At ten years-old it was the name I chose for my first dog. It was the first time I fell instantly in love, and I was head over heels, or paws rather.

I took Snoopy everywhere I could. I fed him twice a day, picked up his crap in the backyard, whatever he needed. We were best friends. I felt great pride in having my own dog. The neighbors along our street would smile, or wave and say "hello" as I walked him on his leash along the sidewalk several times a day. It didn't get much cuter; a cute little reddish-brown-haired boy with a Beatles haircut, walking his puppy on a spring day.

Me at ten years old in front of my Mom's Chevy Impala

We'd play on the front lawn of our house. Snoopy would chase me all around. I'd fall to the ground and he'd jump on me and lick my face as I laughed and playfully pushed him off. We'd play tug-of-war with an old cotton dish towel I found in the kitchen. His little teeth would bite down on the towel and I'd pull him along the grass. He had a good grip. In the backyard we'd play fetch the stick, which he did quite well for being so young. I'd climb up the tree and he'd bark at me as I sat on a large branch half way up and looked down at him on the grass below. He'd attempt to climb up after me, his tiny paws scratching at the tree bark. He was precious. He made me so happy. The happiest I'd ever been in my young life.

Snoopy slept on an old blanket on the floor in my bedroom, at the side of my bed. He was a well-behaved pup. I was able to imitate his puppy whine perfectly, and as a future stand-up comedian and voice actor, this was probably my first animal impression. To this day, I can still sound exactly like a whining puppy. Sometimes I'd wake up in the middle of night and for fun I would do the puppy whine. Snoopy's ears would perk up and he'd look at me confused, as if he were unsure where the sound was coming from. My mom would assume it was Snoopy whining. She'd yell from the other room for me to, "Shut that damn dog up!" I would laugh. Later, I told her it was me and showed her how I made the noise. She didn't think it was funny.

At school, during lunch time, we could either eat our lunch in the cafeteria, or if we lived close by, go home for lunch. Mom wasn't working at the time, and we lived two short blocks from the school, so every day at noon I'd run home to play with Snoopy and eat lunch. It was a joyous time. My first time experiencing unconditional love and I loved the feeling more than anything.

Time with my beloved Snoopy didn't last very long. I remember the day *it* happened, but I don't like to think about *it* too much, because the pain raises *its* very ugly head and *it* still hurts all over again. Okay. Here goes the *it*...

It was late spring. The school lunch bell rang at John J. Bagley Elementary. Time to go home; time to play with Snoopy and eat lunch. I walked out the front entrance, pushing the heavy wooden double-doors out of my way, ran across Curtis Street and down Roselawn Street. I ran for two blocks until I arrived at our house. I jumped up the four small concrete porch steps, opened the front door, entered, and closed it behind me, like many times before.

But this time, something was wrong. Snoopy was not there to greet me. I called him, "Here Snoopy, here Snoopy!" Again, "Here Snoopy, here Snoopy!" I called him several more times to no response. I looked in my bedroom, he wasn't there. In the other bedroom...not there. In my parents' bedroom...not there. In the backyard...not there. In the basement...not there. I was in a panic. I went into the kitchen. Mom was seated at the kitchen table. She had my lunch ready. Food was the last thing on my mind. I stammered out, "W-w-where's Snoopy?" She paused for a moment, looked down at the floor, then back at me and firmly stated, "Your father took him away."

From the tone of her voice I knew what she meant. Snoopy was gone...gone forever. I can't begin to tell you how or what I felt. I was in shock, disbelief. I was dumbfounded. "Why? Why?" I cried. Mom got defensive and curt with me and said I had not taken good care of him like I promised.

I yelled back, "I did too!" with tears rolling down my face. She didn't seem to care. I was being blamed for something I didn't do—a lame, made-up excuse for them to get rid of my puppy.

I was a ten year-old boy who had done everything asked of him concerning his dog. I would have raked leaves, shoveled snow, washed their car—anything to keep my Snoopy and they knew it. I screamed, "I hate you! I hate you! I hate you!" at the top of my lungs. Conflicting feelings of anger, confusion, and sorrow flowed through me. I was numb. I ran into my bedroom, plopped down on my bed, and cried my heart out.

Part of my memory is blank after that moment, except for me crying for several days, yelling at my parents, and telling them I hated them. They never explained to me beyond their lie that it was my fault Snoopy was gone. It may sound strange, but you could probably compare this episode in my childhood to a sort of post-traumatic stress syndrome. I never trusted my parents again, or liked dogs very much after that. There was nothing I could do about it. I had no choice, but to get through it the best I could. I went about life, doing what ten year-olds did; schoolwork, watching TV, and hanging out with my friends. It took me thirty years before I would love another dog.

A couple months later, in late July, the infamous 1967 Detroit riot occurred. I can still see the dirty black smoke in the sky from the burning buildings on Livernois Avenue, less than a mile from our house. It wasn't as bad as what had taken place in Bubbie Sarah's neighborhood. No one explained to me what was going on from any logical or thought-provoking point of view. All I got from my father was a bunch of racist remarks about black people. I didn't pay any attention to him. All my friends were black and none of them were anything like he described. Even at ten I knew my father was not very smart.

I went back to school after summer break. Talk about the riot was on everyone's lips. It usually came in the form of jokes, teasing, or putdowns. Not that it was a particularly funny subject, but when there is pain in the air you have to laugh.

Overall, 1967 was a fun and tragic time in my life. I liked being ten. However, the neighborhood was changing. Crime and violence in the area were on the rise. The following year, when it was time for me to enter junior high, we moved further west into Detroit. Our new house was on Pierson Street, between Evergreen Road and Lahser Road, a stone's throw from Eight Mile Road. Eight Mile is a long road. The neighborhood was middle-class and mostly white. For me it was difficult. Except for the few months I spent in Tucson, I had never been around so many white people in my life. It wasn't a bad thing—I mean, I am considered a white guy by most people's standards. I remained in our new neighborhood for the next six-plus years of my life.

-4-

JUNIOR HIGH, HIGH SCHOOL, AND THE DOGS OF MY TEEN YEARS

Being a new kid in a new neighborhood and attending a new school is always uncomfortable. I was a few months shy of turning twelve when the new school year started. I was thin and only four feet, eleven inches tall. Being a small teenage guy, starting junior high amongst a bunch of larger white boys who see you as an easy target, wasn't my idea of a good time. Kids are mean. I know. I used to be one.

My one escape from family life was schoolwork. Obviously, I was obligated to participate in subjects like Math, Home Economics and English. But the one school activity I enjoyed the most was Wood Shop. I loved and still do love Wood Shop. The smell of sawdust is something I've never grown tired of. If they made sawdust cologne, I'd buy it...and I do not like cologne.

I had a knack for making things out of wood. I made lamps, bowls, even a model sailboat, which I still have. Wood Shop was fun. Throughout junior high and all the way through high school, I was a whiz on the wood lathe.

I won several awards for my woodworking projects on a regional level.

I couldn't relate to the kids in this new school. It was like being in Tucson all over again, but with bigger, older, and meaner kids. At least I was used to the weather. Back at John J. Bagley Elementary, I was never afraid of anyone, no matter how big they were. The tough black kids were my friends. I was the cool little white boy who was fun to hang out with. At Taft Junior High, to the tough white kids, I was the short little punk who was easy to mess with.

It wasn't like I was challenged to fight on a daily basis. It was more like pushing and shoving, "You get out of my way when I walk down the hall" kind of attitudes. Plus, in this new neighborhood, I had to deal with a teenage bully down the street from my house, Bruce, who kept me terrified of walking past his house or playing on the street for two years. Bruce was just big and mean. If he saw me walking he'd pull up to me on his bicycle and punch me in the arm, or slap me in the back of the head...and he carried a knife. Not fun.

On numerous occasions at Taft Junior High, I had my books dumped while walking to and from class. Having your "books dumped" is when you hold your books and loose-leaf notebook under one arm—at your side. Some kid sneaks up behind you, pulls down on the top end of your book stack, causing everything to fall out of your arm and go flying down to the floor. You'd run after your stuff and try to pick it up, while other kids would kick it along the hall. You'd be lucky to make it to your next class on time. If I carried my books in front of my chest to counteract it I'd be teased for carrying them "like a sissy." I had to tolerate this and most of the time I couldn't see who was doing it because it happened so fast. Back then there was no such thing as a book bag.

It took three full years until I grew a few inches and got muscles from lifting weights before I got any respect. I was fourteen, and then it was almost time to enter high school.

Henry Ford High School, which I was about to enroll in, was about two and a half miles from Taft Junior High. Roughly 65-percent of the students were black. This felt more like my old elementary schools. I was happy to be there. One good thing happened, which some might call karma—some of the bullies who messed with me at Taft Junior High and *thought* they were tough got their butts seriously beat on the first day of high school. Some of the *real* tough black kids at Henry Ford High did not like these new freshmen's' attitudes. Henry Ford High was rough and I loved it.

There was serious racial tension from time to time, including two full-blown race riots during my time there. Me, I was home free. No one bothered me, and I continued to be a whiz through high school Wood Shop. The Wood Shop teacher, Mr. Walker, a kind, gray-haired former naval officer, was my friend and mentor in woodworking. He also became a father figure to me and helped me cope with my troubled home life, especially the hard times with my father.

During my time in our new neighborhood, my parents took in two dogs. The first was a male named Sandy, a medium-sized Collie mix. He had floppy ears and a brown-and-white coat. My father took him from a friend who said he had found him on the street. My relationship with Sandy was anything but pleasant. I did not like this dog. He used to piss on the couch in the living room and it stunk up the place. I don't like to admit it, but I was mean to him. I still had so much pain about my puppy Snoopy being taken from me four years earlier, and any dog I was around wasn't going to make me happy. I couldn't feel or give any love to an animal, especially a dog. Of course I didn't consciously feel this way at that time. It's my analysis of my teenage years as an adult. Sandy growled at me on several occasions. We both didn't like each other.

My parents asked me to walk him from time to time. I didn't mind. It was a good way to get out of the house, away from the constant yelling which was considered communication in our happy home. Sandy would pull hard when he walked. I'd pull his leash in to get better control and then he'd do his business on the neighbors' lawns. Once we had a little run-in with the grandfather of an acquaintance of mine. The grandfather was part of the Marucci clan, a loud Italian family who lived around the corner. I hung out with Joe, a gawky kid, who was my age.

As Sandy and I passed their house on the corner, we walked along their backyard fence with grape vines growing over it. Sandy lifted his leg and. I didn't think anything of it. All of a sudden, Joe's grandfather comes running around the corner, like some lunatic old man out of a Fellini movie. He screamed, "Don't-a pee on my-a grapes, Don't-a pee on my-a grapes." Before I saw it coming, he kicked Sandy firmly in the side. Sandy howled in pain and I pulled him away. I screamed, "Stop! Leave him alone!" Old man Marucci mumbled something more about his grapes and started swearing at me in Italian. I flipped him the finger and ran with Sandy. I did not want to deal with this crazy old man.

Who grew grapes in their crappy backyard in Detroit? I never walked Sandy past the Marucci's house again.

Sandy seemed okay. The kick to his side wasn't serious. I took him home. My father eventually gave him away, too. At this point, I could not have cared less and was glad he was gone. Who knows where my Father took him? Most likely the city dog pound.

The second dog was Lady, a black and white Brittany Spaniel with a freckled face who couldn't have been more than a year or two old. She was beautiful. This was another dog my father took in from *another* friend who claimed he had snatched it from a neighbor who was abusing her. Thinking about it now, that made no sense because Lady was starved for attention. When you'd come home she would repeatedly jump on you. You'd have to push her away several times to get her to stop and calm down. A dog that was abused or beaten would most likely shy away from people, and be in fear of being hit. Who knows where the dog had really come from? My father's friend, a shyster upholstery salesman co-worker who smelled like cigarettes and always had a glass of whiskey in his hand, might have stolen Lady from someone he didn't like, or found her wandering the streets—any number of scenarios.

Lady, I was kinder to, but still held my distance. She was an extremely fast runner. I enjoyed playing fetch-the-ball with her in the backyard. During the time she was with us, which wasn't more than a few months, I used to find dead sparrows in our backyard. I remember wondering how they had gotten there. Was our crazy next door neighbor shooting them with a bee-bee gun? Then one day I saw Lady catch a sparrow in her teeth before it could leave the ground. I was fascinated. I looked in the encyclopedia and discovered Brittany Spaniels had been bred for bird hunting. Go figure.

Lady had a habit of running away if the backyard gate was left open. If it was open even a couple of inches she'd somehow open it wider and run out. I helped find her once. She had done it several times, and each time we got her back. On her last run we never saw her again. My sister had left the gate open. We looked throughout the neighborhood to no avail. As pretty as Lady was, she most likely was taken in by another family.

To my knowledge my parents never called the dog pounds or animal shelters, or put up flyers, like most people. To them losing a dog was like losing a piece of furniture, only it consumed dog food and now they were off the hook from purchasing anymore. I don't mean to sound so callus about my parents and their treatment of dogs, but they didn't have a very good track record.

There was one dog I actually did like as a teenager. My friend Wayne had an extra stocky, Beagle-American Foxhound mix named Burlo. Wayne, at sixteen, was a badass. He was built like a tank and drove a 1966 305 Honda Superhawk motorcycle. Even though he did not play on any high school sports teams, you did not want to fight Wayne. His dog Burlo was *cool beans*. His personality was so out there—even if you didn't like dogs, you could not ignore Burlo. He'd come running up to you all slobbery and smiling like some animated cartoon dog. On my many visits to Wayne's house, I always petted and played with Burlo. He made me smile.

-5-

DOGS IN HOLLYWOOD

I graduated from Henry Ford High School in Detroit in February of 1974. It would have been a January graduating class; however there was a six-week teacher strike the previous year, so they moved it to February. I turned seventeen a few weeks before graduation. The reason I graduated so young; back then grades one through twelve were divided into As and Bs, grade 7A and 7B made up the 7th grade. If you wanted to move up one half-grade you could go to summer school for eight weeks, take a few mandatory courses, and if you passed, they would move you up. I did it twice and graduated from high school a year earlier. With the exception of Wood Shop I hated school and wanted out as soon as possible. I didn't mind sacrificing a couple summer vacations. I should have done it every summer. I would have graduated high school at twelve.

For about two years, while attending high school, I worked evenings, weekends, and summers in the shipping and receiving department of Robinson Furniture, a high-end furniture store in the adjacent suburb of Southfield, Michigan, several miles from my house. I saved as much money as I could for my move to Hollywood, to become a stand-up comedian. Big dreams and a not so stable home life had lit a fire in me. I was aggressive in my plan. I purchased a blue, 1969 Ford Club Wagon van and drove it to Hollywood, not knowing anyone. Though I had been through a lot in my life, I always tried to find the humor in everything. I was a funny kid who had a true gift for mimicry and an excellent ear for accents and dialects.

Eight months after high school I found myself regularly performing stand-up comedy routines at the World Famous Comedy Store in Hollywood on the Sunset Strip. Actually, back then it wasn't world-famous. I've done that line of work professionally ever since, as well as working as an actor and voice actor—providing voices for cartoons, commercials, movies, and video games.

I worked steadily for many years, doing my stand-up comedy act all over the country and acting in television shows. I rarely had any serious contact with dogs until around 1996. Because of my childhood experiences I had subconsciously put a wall around myself, not befriending anyone with a dog. I still didn't have a fear of them; I just didn't want to get hurt emotionally. When it came to dogs, I was still a ten year-old boy.

One day I met a fellow voice actor, Wanda—a tall, Canadian blonde, who also did part-time nude art modeling. We worked together providing voices for a short-lived cartoon series. I started hanging around her and several of her friends, all animal owners, mostly dogs. Wanda rescued dogs, fostered dogs, and owned several cats. It was the first time I'd heard about rescuing and fostering animals, and I was intrigued by it. I was almost forty and...maybe a little wiser. I needed to be more mature about my issues with dogs.

I still didn't like it when one of their dogs would jump

on me, or breathe its nasty dog-breath in my direction, or beg for my food when I was eating. I didn't show them any love, like I do now. I merely put up with them. I didn't realize then how being an adult dog owner could be one of the greatest joys in life.

One of Wanda's friends, Ken, a long-haired, mellow musician, owned a funny little male Pug named Neptune. One afternoon we were hanging out at a backyard barbeque. I was eating a plate of food and Neptune came running up to me, breathing hard and loud like Pugs do. He sat at my side begging for some of my food. I firmly told him to, "get away from me." Ken heard me. He told Neptune to quit begging and move away...and he did.

In time, as I changed, I found Neptune to be a pretty cool dog. Neptune had an odd habit of messing with the biggest dogs he came in contact with, from Rottweilers to Mastiffs. He'd quickly sneak up behind them and crawl between their hind legs, scaring the crap out of them. The big dog would be thrown off balance and practically trip over itself. Neptune would then bark nonstop at the dog. Ken would then chase Neptune away and apologize to the big dog's owner. It was always fun to see Neptune in action.

Wanda's boyfriend, Craig, a cigarette-smoking vegetarian and also a musician, owned a cute white Chihuahua named Pinch, who was an ornery little bugger to most people other than his owner. Pinch once bit a vet during an examination. He didn't play much with other dogs. He was like a strange lap dog you didn't want to pet. Spending time with these guys and their dogs contributed to me making that life changing decision: to get my first dog in 30 years.

Another group of actors, artistic friends, and acquaintances I hung out with included Tony, a brilliant, flamboyant interior designer, who could make anyone's home or office look incredible. Tony had two very well-groomed Springer Spaniels, both black-and-white. They kind of reminded me of Lady, the Brittany Spaniel, from my teenage years.

Tony was going on a trip for a couple of days and he asked if I would house-sit and watch his two dogs. This was in late August of 1997. I didn't know why he asked me, I didn't think we were that good of friends. We were more like *good acquaintances*. Maybe he couldn't get anyone else. I don't know. But whatever the reason, this seemingly small event changed my life forever.

I agreed. I liked Tony and I liked his dogs. They were sweet. I liked their look and temperament and they seemed to like me. Plus, after hanging around my other group of friends with dogs, I was very open to it.

Tony's home was elegantly decorated in a black and white motif. Everything from black and white tiles on the kitchen floor, to a black and white sofa, loveseat and rug in the living room, to a perfect black and white configuration in the bathroom. I think Tony liked black and white.

During my two day stay, I walked the dogs, fed them, and played with them in the backyard. I was actually having fun. I wasn't full-out dog crazy, but I was okay at this stage of my new-found dog awareness. It wasn't until I went to sleep that I experienced the warmth and comfort these special beings could give.

I was lying in bed, relaxing with the door open. It was a hot August night, and I wanted to get a cool cross-breeze of wind from the open windows in the living room since the house had no air conditioning. I heard the sound of the two dogs walking on the tile floor throughout the house. I then heard a couple of sighs, as they both plopped down in the doorway of the bedroom where I laid.

It was as if they were guarding me, protecting me, their temporary two-day master of the house. I felt comforted. It was a feeling I hadn't felt, or wanted to feel, since I was back in Detroit with my puppy, Snoopy. I fell asleep. I slept well. To my surprise, when I awoke the next morning, the two dogs had not left the doorway. They had been guarding me all night long. I was overwhelmed, my feelings were raw. I was ten again and I liked the feeling. I started to cry. It was a hard cry, a cry of what I missed for the last 30 years, a cry of heartache and happiness rolled into one. It was then *I knew* I would have a dog of my own. I was ready to take on the challenge with all the love I had suppressed for so long.

I rose from bed, petted and fed the dogs. These two Springer Spaniels showed me there was no longer anything to fear emotionally from man's best friend. The ten year old in me was alive again, and he was about to break free.

-6-

GETTING A PUPPY AGAIN

Wanting a dog and actually going out and getting one are two different things. It's a big deal to adopt a dog, no matter what your age. Making a lifetime commitment, or at least for the life of the dog commitment, is serious stuff.

Of course there are dog owners who buy a cute puppy on a whim, get bored with him or her, and a few weeks later get rid of it. Personally, I'd like to see those people punished. Anyhow, before I embarked on getting a new love of my life, I spoke with Wanda. She lectured me about the commitment of owning a dog and everything that went along with it.

As she was speaking I realized it didn't matter what she said. I was confident and committed to finding the right dog for me, giving him, or her, my love and a great home. I would do whatever it took, for however long it took. I was ready.

I knew not to get a puppy from a puppy mill, or a pet shop *claiming* their dogs weren't from puppy mills, and that they bought from well-respected breeders. Breeder or puppy mill, I wasn't having it. I don't have anything against someone running a puppy mill, trying to make a living... wait a minute. Yes, I do. A puppy mill is just wrong. They are cruel places that inhumanely treat dogs. They are breeding factories that exist to produce puppies for profit. Getting a puppy from a puppy mill would be like adopting a child conceived from an unknown sperm donor in a third world country, and having the doctor tell you, "We guarantee all our sperm donors have better bodies than Taylor Lautner, and IQs higher than Albert Einstein." Yeah, right. No thanks, I'll pass.

I decided to get my new dog from the Burbank Animal Shelter in beautiful Burbank, California, where I lived. Burbank is a quaint little city in the suburbs of Los Angeles known as the Valley. I liked it there. Low crime, hardworking everyday people, and some of the streets to this day look like they haven't been touched since the 1950s.

I went to the shelter on Monday, September 8th, 1997. It was my first time at any animal shelter. I didn't know what to expect. At least this one, from what I could see and from what I had been told, was very clean and well-run. I parked my car in the adjoining parking lot. I waited for a moment then exited. I walked about fifty feet to the front entrance and entered the facility through an automatic glass door. The first thing I saw on the wall facing me was a large plaque with a picture of Benji on it, the dog who starred in the self-titled movie *Benji*, as well as *For the Love of Benji*, and *Benji the Hunted.* Underneath his picture it read: Benji, Shelter Super Star. The dog who launched a million adoptions. The Burbank Animal Shelter was where his original owner and trainer, Frank Inn, had found him. Maybe I'd be as lucky in finding a great pooch here too.

Around and within the shelter in cement are the paw prints of famous dogs and the names of their owners and trainers that won Patsy Awards...dogs that starred in movies and television series from the 1940s through 1970s, a sort of mini Grauman's Chinese Theatre of paw prints. From the Yellow Lab in the classic film Old Yeller, to Lassie, to Rin Tin Tin.

I asked the attendant behind the counter about adopting a dog. He pointed to the area where the dogs were kept and stated the fee for adoption was $48.71, and if the dog wasn't neutered, and was four months or older, there would be an additional $30.00 neutering fee. You had to get the dog neutered before you could take possession, which I assumed was a city or county law. He also told me if there was a dog I wanted to possibly adopt, he would have him, or her, taken out of their kennel and brought to an outside area so we could get acquainted. I thanked him for the information and proceeded down the hall and through a tan door. This took me outside the building. I walked about ten feet to another building with another tan door. I could hear the cries and noises of various dogs inside. The kind of cries and noises they make when they are housed in unfamiliar surroundings.

I entered. As I walked along the cement floor the faint smell of dog urine and feces hit my nose. The kennels were open aired but some smell was bound to remain there. Kennels on both sides of me contained the dogs up for adoption, some were one to a kennel; some two in a kennel. The dogs were of various ages, breeds and sizes; mostly mixed breeds, and quite a few were on their last stop before euthanasia. Part of the adoption process is very sad.

A slip of paper was clipped to every kennel with each dog's intake information. It contained the kennel number, the date the dog had arrived, its color, its breed or mix of breeds, when the dog was available to adopt, and the name, address and phone number of the person who had brought them to the shelter.

I walked along one side of kennels looking at the various dogs. There were a few old Pit Bull mixes, a very old purebred Rottweiler and several small, ratty-looking mixed breeds you could tell the owners had abandoned so they wouldn't have to deal with mounting veterinarian bills... poor babies. Of course I didn't have this sort of awareness of animals back then; this is my point of view thinking about it in retrospect.

As I walked along the other row of kennels behind me, I stopped at kennel number eighteen and came upon the dog who would be my best friend for the next thirteen-plus years of our lives. He was a brown-and-white furry puppy with three-quarters of his front legs looking like he was wearing a pair of bright white, furry socks. He had pointed ears like a cute little fox and a perfectly shaped snout—not too long, not too short—with a cute, sensitive black nose. He was considered a medium-sized dog. His tail was slightly bushy and he weighed 22 pounds.

His intake information identified him as a four-to-five month old Collie-Shepherd mix. I would soon discover he was a Sheltie mixed most likely with American Eskimo, which I later found out are two very smart breeds. Shelties are very sweet dogs. They're officially known as Shetland Sheepdogs, originating from Scotland and bred as herding dogs to herd sheep. I slipped my fingers through the kennel wires and he licked them, which caused me to laugh and smile.

He was the prettiest dog I had ever seen. Plus, there was

something about his eyes. They were dark brown like many dogs, but what was behind them is what stood out. It's hard to describe in words, you would have had to have him look at you, like he looked at me. It was as if he had soft, gentle human eyes. Eyes that said, "Hello...I love you...I'll never hurt you...I'll be your friend no matter what." After that look I knew I needed to have this sweet creature in my life. Throughout the years his eyes never wavered with the love I felt on that very first day, and he gave it unconditionally with every breath he took.

Inside the kennel standing next to him was a much smaller and older dog, which wasn't well taken care of. I can't remember too much about him because when I saw my pooch I fell instantly in love.

I grabbed the slip of paper with his intake information, took it back to the main building of the shelter and presented it to the attendant behind the counter. I told him I wanted to have this Collie-Shepherd mix taken out of his kennel so we could get acquainted—I wanted to adopt him. He told me to wait outside the building that housed the dogs; he would have someone bring the dog out. I anxiously went outside and stood in a grassy area waiting for my soon-to-be puppy.

Less than two minutes passed. Another attendant walked out with the pup and handed me his leash. I was *ecstatic*. The puppy's tail was wagging wildly; he was a ball of love. I kneeled down to pet him and he kissed me all over. I think most people call it that when a dog keeps licking them. Whether it's technically what they are doing, I don't know. I liked it, but I was a little taken aback by it. It had been 30 years since I had let a dog get this close.

Though I befriended other people's dogs, I still kept

some distance, physically and emotionally. This was different—this puppy was special—like meeting someone with undeniable charisma.

I hung out with him for about ten minutes. He was so happy to be out of his kennel. His intake information stated he would be available for adoption the following morning, Tuesday, September 9, 1997, at 8:00. It would make seven days he had been at the shelter, and no one claimed him. Seven days was the waiting period. I said goodbye to the puppy and thanked the attendant. He took him back to his kennel and I left, vowing to be back at 8:00 the following morning to adopt him. It was time for a new journey in my life.

-7-

THE PUPPY I ALMOST DIDN'T GET

I was revved up with excitement. My mind was racing 100 miles an hour. I was going to get a puppy. Me with a new puppy. I couldn't remember being this excited about anything. WOW! Simply, WOW! I went to the pet store and purchased a dog collar, a leash, puppy dog chow, dog bowls, and some doggie toys for him to chew on. I also bought a newspaper since I didn't know if he was house broken or not.

Plus, I purchased a large dog crate. I was told by my group of dog friends that it might be a good idea to crate train a puppy. That night I couldn't sleep. I tossed and turned, thinking about having a dog in my life—the responsibility, being vulnerable, allowing a dog's love again.

Morning came. I ate breakfast, grabbed my pup's new collar and leash, and was out the door. The Burbank Animal Shelter was a few miles from my apartment, about a ten minute drive. I left early and got there about 7:40, and waited in my car in the parking lot. I'm a stickler for always being on time, so I'm usually early—it's one of my pet peeves. Around 7:50, a burgundy pickup truck pulled in the lot, several spaces from my car. It was the only other vehicle in the lot besides mine, so it was easy to notice. The guy inside was a nondescript white guy around my age, wearing a baseball cap. At 7:55, I exited my car, walked to the front entrance and waited for them to open up. An attendant opened the door at 8:00 sharp.

To my surprise, the person on the other side of the door was my neighbor who lived around the corner. I didn't really know her. I saw her from time to time, walking her dog, and we would exchange hellos. I didn't even know her name, or that she worked there. We officially introduced ourselves. Her name was Claudia. She was glad I was adopting a dog. Claudia was a red-haired woman in her early-fifties with a slight toughness—like a former biker chick that got out of the life—with a heart of compassion underneath. After all, anyone who worked in an animal shelter for fifteen years—as I later found out—had to have a good heart, at least when it came to animals.

I headed through the two tan doors once again. There was my pup in kennel number eighteen, looking as beautiful as he had the day before. He whined a sort of "hello" as if he knew I was coming for him. I smiled and said, "Hello, Puppy...you've got a new home." I grabbed the slip of paper with his intake information so I could take care of the adoption paperwork.

All of a sudden, I felt a presence beside me. I look to my left. It was the guy from the parking lot in the pickup truck. He said, "Hi." I said, "Hello." He said he was also there to adopt *this* dog. That he and his wife had come to the shelter four times to visit him. My heart sank and I firmly stated, "I want him, too!" Of all the dogs he could have chosen, this guy had to want the same dog as me.

We proceeded to the front counter. There stood Claudia. I explained our predicament. She said it happened all the time. Several people often wanted to adopt the same pet. She told us there was a purebred Rottweiler puppy up for adoption a while back, and twenty people wanted it. She did with them what she was about to do with us—have a drawing. At least I had a fifty-fifty chance. She pulled out a roll of tickets, like the ones you get at a fundraiser when they do a raffle. She tore off two, broke them in half at the perforated mark in the center, and gave us each one of the halves. She put the matching halves in a wide-mouth glass jar kept under the counter.

My heart was racing as she covered the jar with its lid. She shook it up, removed the lid, reached in, and grabbed one of the ticket halves. She read the number. It was mine. The puppy was mine. I won. YAY! Three cheers for me! I breathed a sigh of relief. The guy with the pickup truck graciously left. I didn't feel bad for him. There were many other dogs to adopt. I wanted the pup and I got him. *It was meant to be.* I named my new puppy Snoopy, in honor of the puppy I'd had as a boy. When I would tell people my new pup's name, most would say, "How cute." Younger people would say, "Oh, like Snoop Doggy Dogg?" I'd always reply, "He's not named after that jerk. It's **Snoopy** like Snoopy from *Peanuts*, the Charles Schultz character."

I paid the pet-adoption fee, neutering and license fees, and filled out some paperwork. Snoopy was set to be neutered later in the day. I was told I could pick him up at 4:00 that afternoon at the Burbank Animal Hospital. It was about a half mile down the road, on the same side of the street as the shelter. I said goodbye and thanks to Claudia, then a quick goodbye to Snoopy, and told him I'd see him later that day. I went out to my car in the parking lot, sat behind the steering wheel, and wept. I cried loud and hard, I was overwhelmed. I couldn't believe I'd gotten a dog after all these years. I was finally facing my issues about dogs. I was extremely happy—happy again for once in my life. I composed myself and went home.

Snoopy's intake information and relinquishment record

My mind goes blank when I try to remember what I did until late afternoon. All I remember was showing up at the Burbank Animal Hospital a few minutes before 4:00 to pick up my pup. I wouldn't have chosen that animal hospital to get him neutered. They obviously had some kind of arrangement with the shelter.

The place didn't feel right. It looked old and bland. The furniture in the front office looked like it had been there since the 1950s and had never been moved. It wasn't just the décor, the employees seemed lackadaisical and bored, like they were only working there to get a paycheck, not because they had a passion for animals. The girl behind the counter was cold and robotic. I showed her Snoopy's paperwork. She buzzed someone on the intercom and told them I was there to pick up my dog.

I waited several minutes and a vet tech brought Snoopy out. He seemed happy to see me, his tail wagged a little. The vet tech told me he was sore from the surgery and stitches, and a little groggy from the sedative, and not to walk him very much in the coming days. Made sense to me. Remove anyone's testicles and give them drugs, and they'll definitely be sore and groggy.

The vet tech wanted me to make an appointment to bring Snoopy back in one week to take out his stitches. I told him I needed to get going and I'd call him later to schedule it. The vibe I got from those folks...I wouldn't let them park my car, let alone touch my dog again. I made arrangements with another Burbank veterinarian I found at the VCA Animal Hospital to take out Snoopy's stitches, Dr. Sheldon Altman, who turned out to be a class act.

-8-

SNOOPY'S NEW HOME

My two-bedroom apartment was on the second floor of an older wood and stucco, four-unit building around the corner from Warner Brother's movie studio in Burbank, on Kenwood Street. Following the post-surgery recommendation, I carried Snoopy up and down the stairs for a few days. Poor baby. The large crate I bought to "crate train" him in was a total waste of money. I put Snoopy in it and I could see he was uncomfortable. Within a minute he pissed himself. After being in a kennel in a shelter for seven days the last thing he wanted was to be caged-up in his new home. Out to the garage it went.

Snoopy didn't bark for the first week or so. I'm not sure why. He could have been nervous from the stress of moving around, his surgery, or being in a new environment. He sure made up for it after he got comfortable. Snoopy turned out to be a great watchdog, which was a plus, since my apartment had no real security. His bark was strong and effective. If you were outside my apartment and heard his bark you would assume a much larger dog was inside.

I was glad he was only half Sheltie. Numerous articles I read stated that purebred Shelties were notorious barkers.

Some people have their Shelties "debarked," a surgical procedure that involves removing tissue from a dog's vocal cords, resulting in their bark sounding more like a whisper. This is cruel. These so-called dog owners should be punished by being tied down and having *their* vocal cords removed without anesthesia, so *they* can shut up and leave the sweet Shelties alone.

I became fascinated with my new best friend. Though he was now mine, I still wanted to know more about him, where he came from. I looked for the name and phone number of the person that had brought Snoopy to the shelter on his intake information. His name was Brad. I wanted to thank him and let him know, Snoopy now had a good home. I called the number. It was in the 818 area code, meaning he was also somewhere in the Valley. The phone rang a few times. A man answered, it was Brad. I introduced myself and told him I was now the owner of the dog he had dropped off at the Burbank Animal Shelter. I heard the smile in his voice and he said, "You mean, Wolfie?" I said, "I named him Snoopy." He called him Wolfie, because Snoopy did look sort of like a fox, or a brown and white wolf, if there is such a thing.

Brad proceeded to tell me he had found Snoopy wandering around his backyard, in Shadow Hills, which is an area north of Burbank near the Tujunga Valley. He said Snoopy was covered in so much dirt and dried mud; he washed him twice to see what he really looked like. He must have been wandering around out there for several days. Brad fed him and decided not to keep him because he already owned a dog, and didn't want another. Shadow Hills has many ranch-type homes and horse stables amongst grungy farmland...and coyotes.

Snoopy was lucky he had not gotten eaten by coyotes. Taking him to the shelter had been the right thing to do. Maybe his owner would claim him, or a child was missing his beloved pup. What kind of moron would abandon a dog like this? If there are different kinds of morons, this person was a new breed. There was no way a dog this loyal and well-behaved would run away from his owner. At this point I didn't care. All I knew was, he was now mine and I would give him the best life I could. I thanked Brad again and hung up the phone.

Most people like to think their dogs are smart. However, various breeds have different levels of intellect. Borzoi or Afghan hounds aren't known for their remarkable intelligence. They can be pretty dogs, but if they were given the equivalent of a doggy I.Q. test or an S.A.T. they wouldn't be at the top of the class.

Snoopy, on the other hand, was extremely well-behaved and very smart. I'm not saying this because Shelties are in the top-ten list of smartest dogs, or because I loved my new pup. He truly was a special animal. I lucked into it. For instance, he was housebroken within one week. I no longer needed to have newspaper in the kitchen area for him to pee or poop on. Within three weeks I was able to have him off-leash and walking alongside me in back of my apartment building. No worries about him running away. He did, however, have to be on-leash for walks around the block. He would never run in the street, but depending on the time of year, he loved to chase squirrels. Having him on-leash was the best option.

Coming from a shelter and having a background I knew very little about, you would think there would be behavioral issues. None that I could see. He wasn't skittish or fearful of his new environment, or people; he was an all-around sweet boy.

He was also very intuitive, almost psychic. He would know when I was going to be away for part of the day and wouldn't drink his water. I'd come home after being gone for several hours and his water bowl would be as full as I had left it in the morning. After greeting me with his wildly-wagging tail, and plenty of kisses, he'd drink his water and then I'd take him outside for a walk to do whatever business he needed to do.

His intuitiveness about people over the years caused him to growl at an auto mechanic who was trying to rip me off, and bark and growl at a mentally unbalanced woman he didn't want me to be around. He also barked and growled at a five year old girl; I later found out she was a problem child like in the movie *The Bad Seed*.

Having a dog come into my life was a great learning experience. It was as if I had adopted a baby. A baby from the animal world that I was responsible for on a daily basis. A domesticated dog is not self-reliant like other animals in the wild. It needs tender loving human care throughout its life. I took on this responsibility with great care and enthusiasm, and it never left me all the time we were together. I realize many people who have kids and no pets can't relate to someone like me. I'd be considered an animal loving nut of some kind, someone obsessed about his dog.

Well, not from my point of view. Having kids was not in the cards for me. My friend Barrie put it this way. He said, "The part of the brain that gets switched on, the maternal connection, when you have a kid was never activated in you, so Snoopy became your kid." I liked his observation. It put in perspective my deep emotional response to Snoopy. As far as I was concerned, he was my kid. I'd have killed anyone who would have intentionally hurt him, or at least made sure they were hurting pretty good. It would have been hard to control myself if something like that happened. Thankfully, I was never put in that situation.

As the quote by author and animal enthusiast Roger Caras goes, "Dogs are not our whole life, but they make our lives whole." That quote sums up only *partly* how I felt about my dog. Snoopy gave me new life. He opened my life up to a new world of loving and caring. He helped me become less of a self-absorbed person. He taught me the world does have magic in it when you help another creature, a creature who loves you more than you could possibly love yourself.

Snoopy teething on a Frisbee...our first week together

-9-

SNOOPY'S FIRST GROOMING

After ten days or so of being together, while petting and playing with Snoopy, I felt little bumps underneath his fur. As I looked closer, I discovered a dozen or more, brown, pimple-like dots, protruding out of his skin and spread all over his body. They were about an eighth of an inch wide, and a quarter inch or more in length. I pulled one out with my forefinger and thumb, which caused him some discomfort. I noticed a tiny bit of blood on his skin. What the heck were these things? I had no clue. I knew he wasn't sick, he was his playful puppy self. I decided to take him to a groomer.

It would be my first time dealing with a groomer. I called around and found one with a good rep and a good price in North Hollywood, California, on Laurel Canyon Boulevard, not too far from my apartment. I got a same-day appointment and arrived on time. The shop was clean, the atmosphere pleasant. In addition to providing pet grooming services they also sold high-end dog food and various doggie accessories. We were greeted with words I would continue to hear for the rest of his life, "Oh, he's so pretty."

I learned the little brown bumps were ticks; little bloodsucking leech-like critters who liked to crawl onto warm-blooded furry animals. Most dog owners would have known this at first glance, but I was new to the game. The groomer said Snoopy most likely got them from being around the Shadow Hills area he came from, or from being in the shelter. Not a big deal, she could get rid of them—no problem. These little suckers needed to go. Now knowing what they were and that they weren't life threatening, I was relieved.

The groomer, who was also the owner of the shop, was a middle-aged woman with a sort of homespun quality. She was extremely kind and nurturing. It was obvious she loved her job, and most of all dogs. I ordered Snoopy a bath, the removal of the ticks, of course, a flea dip just in case, and a nail trim. I was told I had to leave him for a couple hours, which I wasn't expecting. I had never left him with anyone at this point, other than the people at the animal hospital, but I got a great vibe from the woman, so I agreed.

When I arrived back at the grooming shop, Snoopy was brought out, and he looked gorgeous. His fur was clean, bright and shiny, combed and fluffed out like a show dog... his tail wagging wildly. I greeted him with a hug and a kiss. The groomer told me, he had been very well-behaved, but the noise of the blow dryer, while being brushed out after his bath, literally scared the crap out of him. He pooped all over the grooming table. Poor baby.

I paid the woman her fee, and as we were leaving she wanted to give Snoopy a special doggy treat. I said "okay." She handed me a dried pig's ear. A dried pig's ear? Wasn't that part of the pig you were supposed to throw away? I guess not. What a slimy disgusting thing. Plus, me being a vegan, it really grossed me out. Turns out dogs love them. Snoopy went crazy as she handed it to me, jumping up, trying to get it. It smelled terrible, but to dogs it must be better than chocolate. I had her put it in a bag, and I took it and Snoopy home.

I gave him the dried pig's ear back at the apartment. He loved it and devoured it as quickly as he could. I later found out how *really* disgusting this thing was. The next day, when I took him for a walk, he pooped it out...it was like liquid mush. It got all over his furry butt. I had to wash it off so he wouldn't ruin my carpet. I'm glad Snoopy enjoyed it because it was the first and *only time* he ate a dried pig's ear.

-10-

DOG CLASS

Snoopy's obedient demeanor was there from the very beginning. I could be talking to someone on the street and within a minute he would start sniffing the ground around me, then lay gently at my feet. I can't begin to count the times people would comment on his behavior and say things like, "Boy, I wish my dog was like him," "He's *soooo* well-behaved," "How'd you get him to do that?" and on and on.

I never taught him that—it came naturally. The first week I had him I was able to teach him to sit and to give me his paw on command. I've never understood people who ask a dog for its paw and think the dog is somehow greeting them with a handshake. The dog *is not* shaking hands with you. It's most likely a playful gesture. If a dog wanted to greet you, *like a dog*, it'd sniff you, or bury its nose in the crack of your butt.

I enrolled Snoopy in a dog training class three weeks after I adopted him. I wanted him to learn the basics...stay, rollover, come, lay down, etc. So, I signed him up for an eight-week course; eight, 90 minute classes on Saturday mornings, at a park in Glendale, California, a few miles from Burbank. The instructor and trainer, Bill, was a gentle man in his fifties who looked like a character actor out of an old movie western...and his price was right. Only 60 bucks for the full course. The thing I liked best about this class was that *the dog owner* did the training, meaning you would do what Bill did with his dog—with your dog. It wasn't one of those dog training places where you let the trainer teach your dog new behaviors and tricks and then he only listens to the trainer—not you. This was hands-on fun.

There were about fifteen dogs and their owners in the class. The dogs ranged from a German Shepherd, to a Poodle, to Mutts of Unknown Origin. Everyone in class would form a single-file line with their dog on-leash. Bill would stand several yards from us with his dog, a mellow, older Golden Retriever. He'd then demonstrate the trick or behavior he wanted our dogs to learn, with his dog. For example, if he wanted us to teach our dogs to roll over, we'd repeat the movements and commands he gave his dog—to our dogs.

It was a lot of fun. I was up every Saturday morning with my puppy playing in a park. Life was good. Snoopy took to these training exercises like a duck takes to water. It was so easy for him—too easy. I knew he was smart, but he surprised me how quickly he learned. He remembered the moves after only two or three tries. I had a little something to do with it, since I have a loud commanding voice, which he responded to quite nicely. Plus, he wanted to please his new master. Snoopy was so good that on a couple of occasions Bill singled him out to the other dog owners as an example of how certain movements and commands should be done. Once he took hold of Snoopy's leash to demonstrate how a correct *sit and stay* should be done. Snoopy did it perfectly. Bill praised him and handed me back his leash. I was a proud new poppa and loved every minute of it.

The training was a good thing. I put what Snoopy learned into practice right away with things like having him sit at the street corner when we encountered a stop light while on a walk, or having him roll over for a biscuit—fun little things. And he never forgot what he learned over the years.

They say—although I don't know who *they* is—you can't teach an old dog new tricks. Well, I beg like a dog to differ. When Snoopy was ten years old, and according to various charts, anywhere from 60-66 in equivalent human years, I taught him trigonometry, how to fly a helicopter, and how to make sushi. Truly amazing!

-11-

SNOOPY MEETS ADELAIDE

I wanted to show off Snoopy as though he were my newborn son. In my eyes being the owner of a wonderful dog was the next best thing, if not better.

My friend Teresa, a very funny comedic actress and dog lover, had a female Cocker Spaniel named Adelaide. I had not had Snoopy more than a few weeks and wanted to see how he would react to other dogs, so I asked if I could bring him over for them to meet. Teresa was fine with it, but she let me know Adelaide was an older dog, ten or so, and she wasn't too playful with other dogs.

Snoopy and I arrived at Teresa and Adelaide's house in North Hollywood for a visit. Snoopy, full of puppy energy, greeted them with great enthusiasm. Teresa petted him and got a kick out of how cute and playful he was. He barked at Adelaide and ran around her in circles signaling he wanted to play. She could care less that he was there. Adelaide was a very sweet Cocker, but had no urge to run around the house with my pup. She was set in her ways, moved at her own pace, and wasn't about to change for anyone, or any dog, who happened to visit. Kind of like a cat.

However, she did take extreme interest in her food

49

like any other dog. Adelaide ate very slowly, nibbling at her bowl of dry food a little at a time throughout the day at a leisurely pace until it was gone, also like a cat. Snoopy, on the other hand, ate very fast. He was still growing and was up for eating as much dry food and biscuits as I'd portioned out for him in any given day. He had no boundaries when it came to eating, whether it was his or any other dog's food.

After Adelaide's refusal to play, Snoopy found one of her chew toys on the carpet, a cow's hoof, which I found almost as disgusting as a dried pig's ear. He grabbed it and started chewing on it. Sweet Adelaide didn't know what to do, or what to make of this energetic boy who was on her turf and doing as he pleased. Teresa found their interactions rather funny. I pried the nasty cow's hoof out of Snoopy's mouth and let Teresa take it out of sight.

Snoopy then ran around the house checking out the rooms and whatever was in them. When he spotted Adelaide's dog food bowl in the kitchen, almost completely full, nothing in the world existed but that food. He started chowing-down on it like he was at home.

Adelaide rushed over and looked at him like, "What the hey?" as he started to scarf her kibble down without a care in the world. The look on Adelaide's face was precious. I grabbed Snoopy by his collar, pulled him away from the bowl, and yelled "no." Then to our surprise, Adelaide went over to her bowl and gobbled-up what was left in a matter of seconds. She then glanced over at Snoopy with a look of, "Nice try, but you won't be eating any of my food again." I started to apologize for Snoopy's etiquette, not that dogs really have etiquette, but Teresa was too busy laughing to hear me. When she caught her breath, she told me she couldn't remember the last time Adelaide ate that fast, if ever. Seems there was no way sweet Adelaide was going to share her grub with my young pup, or any other dog.

-12-

VERDUGO PARK, TENNIS BALLS, AND THE KIDDIE SLIDE

One of the first places I took Snoopy as a pup was Verdugo Park in Burbank; on California Street, near Verdugo Avenue. Snoopy loved this park, and so did I. They had a recreational facility with a community swimming pool, enclosed tennis courts, picnic tables, acres of green grass, and a children's area, with swings, monkey bars and slides. We went there regularly for over nine years. The first couple of months we'd play on the tennis courts. I would let Snoopy run around off-leash and chase tennis balls. I didn't want to take him to dog parks to socialize him with other dogs just yet. He was getting a series of vaccination shots and I was told by Dr. Altman he shouldn't have contact with dogs I didn't know until he was fully vaccinated. That was the only set of shots I ever gave Snoopy. I later found out about the poisons that are used in making vaccines.

Most rabies vaccines contain toxic chemicals like Thimerosal, which contains 49.6 percent mercury, formaldehyde, aluminum hydroxide and other poisonous substances. I decided vaccines were not a good thing to put in Snoopy's body to compromise his immune system. When it came time for him to get the recommended rabies shot every few years, which was required in Burbank to get a dog license, I would lie and tell the vet Snoopy has a bad reaction to it, that he throws up within seconds after it's administered. The vet would say no problem and sign a waiver. To me it was better to lie than to poison my baby. I refused to buy into the fear.

Anyhow, we had a blast playing on the tennis courts. I'd throw a tennis ball over the net. Snoopy would chase after it and put it in his mouth. He was still teething and he'd chew on the ball. For whatever reason, Snoopy did not play fetch. I'd have to run after him, pull the ball from his mouth, and throw it again. We'd play like this for a half hour or so. We did this for several weeks, until it was safe to take him to dog parks. It was great fun. I later discovered he was eating the fuzz off the tennis balls. I didn't notice it at first, but I began to see tennis ball fuzz, or whatever it's called, in his poop. Yellow fuzz can't be good for you. No more tennis balls.

In the children's area of the park I'd let Snoopy off-leash. He loved this area most of all. Kids and their moms never seemed to mind. Snoopy's energy was calm and peaceful. Most people would notice it right away. Some parents would let their shy toddlers, or extremely young babies, pet him to get over their fear of dogs. Of course, I would supervise.

I was always very careful with the little boys, who were about two to five years-old. Sometimes they could be unruly. I would tell them to *pet him nice*, don't touch or pull his tail, and keep away from his face. Then they would gently pet his back or the top of his head. I'd reinforce Snoopy by telling him what a good boy he was and give him a biscuit afterwards.

The children's slide has given me wonderful memories. It was tan and brown and blue, made of hard plastic and steel, about six feet high with *stairs* instead of a ladder, which could be dangerous for small children. For some reason Snoopy seemed drawn to it. I showed him how to get up the stairs the first time. He stopped at the top of the slide. With a little coaxing, and the reward of a biscuit, he slid down to the sand below. WOW! Then he did it again, and again and again. It was wild. He would repeatedly run up the stairs and slide down. If kids were nearby and they saw him do this they couldn't believe their eyes. They'd run over to me and ask his name, and ask if they could pet him.

Snoopy got to the point where once he was off-leash near the slide he'd run up it while kids were playing on it. He'd be right there with 'em, like he was one of them. I always enjoyed seeing the look on their faces when he would do this. Some were taken aback and I'd have to tell them, "It's okay, he won't hurt you," and explain how he liked to go up and down the slide. Some kids would yell to their parents to "watch the doggie on the slide." I never tired of taking Snoopy to Verdugo Park.

It was also a place I'd go to read, work on one of my screenplays, or do some journaling. I'd sit at one of the stone or aluminum picnic tables. At first, Snoopy would lie on the ground next to me, which I didn't like. I didn't want any bugs or ticks to get on him. I'd give the command,

"Snoopy, up!" and he'd jump up onto the picnic table and lay a couple feet from me. It was comforting to have him so close. Snoopy's agility was fantastic. It seemed as if I had adopted some sort of circus dog. He never failed to amaze me and bring warm smiles to my face.

Snoopy playing on the kiddie slide

-13-

RAW KNUCKLEBONES

Our veterinarian, Dr. Altman, was a smart, caring man in his late-sixties, with a world of knowledge in the veterinary field. The first time he saw Snoopy was to take out the stitches from his neutering, which went smoothly. For being so cooperative, Dr. Altman gave Snoopy a beef-flavored doggie treat, which he quickly gobbled down. I then turned to Snoopy and said, "You see, Snoopy, I told you, you needed a good Jewish doctor." Dr. Altman laughed.

Snoopy had gotten kennel cough from being in the shelter for seven days. It was cleared up with antibiotics. I asked Dr. Altman what would be a good way to clean Snoopy's teeth. I didn't buy into the whole "get your dog's teeth cleaned professionally every six months to a year thing" and he agreed. He suggested I get raw knucklebones from a local butcher. They were relatively inexpensive, and they did a great job of cleaning tartar and debris from a dog's teeth. Plus, their bone marrow was supposed to be good for our four-legged friends.

I called several butcher shops in the Burbank area and found one that sold raw knucklebones. Snoopy was a medium-sized dog so I bought two medium-sized bones. I wondered why they were called knucklebones. They aren't from the knuckles of a cow. I don't think cows have knuckles, just hooves. Maybe someone named it that because part of the bone looks like human knuckles in a fist. After a little research I found out the knucklebone is the bone that joins the knee cap in the hind quarter of the cow.

Anyhow, I took the knucklebones home to Snoopy. When I walked through the front door he smelled them through the butcher bag and jumped all over me. Since the bones were raw and untreated they still had a bit of fatty-slimy meat coating on them. I wasn't about to let him eat them on the kitchen floor, or the carpet. I took one out of the bag. Snoopy's whole body perked up. I smiled and in my goofy dog owner's voice said, "Look what Snoopy's getting!" He jumped up on his hind legs trying to get at it as I opened the door to the cement balcony outside my apartment. He whined and followed me outside, his tail wagging happily. I placed the raw knucklebone on the cement slab and he was on it like a hungry hobo on a ham sandwich.

I had seen Snoopy go crazy for a dried pig's ear, beef-flavored treats, a cow's hoof, and various kinds of dog biscuits. But these raw knucklebones must be like super sweet candy to dogs...at least they were to mine. He loved gnawing on this bone more than anything. You could call his name, bring out his leash for him to take a walk, which he loved, bring out his favorite chew toys, whatever. He wasn't moving from his bone.

He gnawed, tore, licked, chomped and bit at his bone for a good half hour, and I decided it was enough. I reached down to take the remainder of it. He could eat what was left of it at another time. I said, "Okay, Snoopy, that's enough for now." My hand moved slightly in the direction of the bone. I heard a faint but firm *grrrr* through his teeth. I moved my hand away, paused for a moment, then moved it back towards the bone. Another *grrrr*, but louder. His sweet eyes gave me a "don't even think about it" look. Here's something I never would've imagined. My sweet boy—the sweetest dog on the planet—the dog so gentle I once watched a butterfly land on his nose as if it were saying "hello" to him—was growling at his master.

I found it rather amusing. He was still so sweet, even when he growled. I smiled, kneeled down next to him and said, "Can I have it, Snoopy?" Another *grrrr*. He wasn't going to bite me, but there was no way he was giving up his bone without a fight. I didn't want him eating the whole thing. It was too much. I didn't want him getting an upset stomach. I looked closer at his teeth and I could see they were cleaner and whiter. The knucklebone was doing what Dr. Altman said it would.

After several minutes, I was getting impatient and a little teed-off. Snoopy would've fought a Rottweiler over the bone. He would have gotten his butt kicked, but there was no doubt he would have tried. I had to trick him to get it. I kneeled down and placed my right hand in front of his face as if I were going to snatch it out of his mouth. He stared at it and made a new noise; *a growling hiss.* With my left hand, I grabbed the back of his dog collar, pulled him up and started moving him around, trying to get him to spit it out. He held onto that knucklebone for dear life. I then tried pulling it out of his mouth with my right hand. After about a minute of me yelling, moving him around, and trying to pull it out, he let go, and it dropped to the cement slab.

I looked down at it. A good three quarters of it was gone. I picked up what was left of the now saliva drenched knucklebone. Snoopy smiled, licked his chops and gave me a look of, "Sorry, I'm a dog. What did you expect?" Then he licked my hand. I smiled and let him back in the apartment. He drank his water bowl dry. I put what was left of the knucklebone in a plastic bag and into the refrigerator. After that incident it was only on rare occasion he got a raw knucklebone, and usually a *small* one, which he would consume in one sitting. After all, they did a great job of cleaning his teeth.

-14-

SNOOPY MEETS MOM AND DAD

In 1986 my parents retired to Southern California. They loved it. The weather was great. No more crappy Detroit winters. They settled in the desert town of Quartz Hill, California, on the border of Lancaster, about 75 miles north of Los Angeles.

I had done my best to forgive them for giving away my puppy so long ago, among other things. But I most definitely could not forget. My mother once told me that she and my father had taken in a puppy a few years after I left for Los Angeles. They had kept the dog for nine years—a new record for them. It may have had something to do with my younger brother, who lived at home for part of that time, taking care of it. She told me they had given the dog away when they moved to California. Seems they had no need to bring along a loving dog they had raised for all those years. For the rest of their lives, they never had any more pets. Maybe that was a good thing.

When I called my mother and told her I had adopted a dog, I'll never forget her response. In a sarcastic tone she said, "*You* got a dog?" Yes, Mom, I got a dog. What I really wanted to say was, "*Took me long enough, don't you think? If you and Dad hadn't messed up my perspective about having pets, maybe I could have had more joy in my life the last thirty years.*" But...there was no need to go there. My mother wasn't a bad or mean person. She was very child-like and naïve in a lot of ways. She married young to get out of the house and had to deal with my controlling father. Part of me felt bad for her.

A couple months after adopting Snoopy, I called Mom and asked if I could bring him out to their place and take her to lunch. She said okay. In her own way, my mom was a dog lover. I knew she'd love my boy.

On a Saturday morning, Snoopy and I arrived at my parent's one bedroom apartment in a senior citizen housing complex. I parked my car outside the small building that housed their unit. I was nervous and excited to introduce them to Snoopy. We entered their apartment; I said "hi" to Mom and Dad and sat on the couch. I let Snoopy off-leash and he ran all around, under the kitchen table, into the bathroom, in and out of the bedroom and living room, then he rested at my feet near the couch.

Mom adored Snoopy. She went gaga over him; calling him every few minutes to come sit near her, "Here Snoopy, here Snoopy!"

Whenever someone other than me would give Snoopy a command and I was present, he would never listen to them, unless I gave a command that it was okay. However, if they had a biscuit or dog treat in hand he would listen to them to get that snack. He loved his treats. I brought some dog biscuits with me and let Mom feed him a couple.

She was like a little girl. It made me smile. It was quite the change from when I was a kid. I never had any type of closure as an adult with my parents, regarding various traumatic issues in my childhood. Whenever I would bring something up, my dad would either avoid the subject or yell in a gruff tone, "Whaddya wanna talk about that for?" and he'd leave the room. Once my dad and I were in a shopping mall and I tried talking to him about something he did to me when I was a kid, and he literally *ran* away from me. I had to run after him and calm him down. I had never seen my dad run before. He wasn't very good at it. He looked like a toddler stumbling over his own feet. It made me laugh.

As my mother was petting Snoopy, I nonchalantly told her I named him after the puppy Uncle Moshe had given me when I was ten. She thought about it for a moment, and said, "Oh, I remember that dog, I hated that dog." She made the remark so flippant, like it was no big deal. I didn't know how to react. There she was going crazy for my *new* puppy named Snoopy, and at the same time, she tells me she hated my *old* puppy named Snoopy. I couldn't believe what I was hearing. How could she be so insensitive? From her body language, which showed a tinge of guilt...and her comment, I realized it was *her* who made the decision to give my puppy away, not my father.

She didn't remember that she had told me, "Your father took him away," thirty years before. I had never forgotten those five words. Dad probably had driven my *old* puppy Snoopy to the city dog pound, or wherever, but mom had made it sound like it was solely my dad's decision, not hers. He was always pretty much a jerk when I was a kid, so it made sense he was the decision-maker on that one. No. It had been Mom. I didn't say anything more about it. What was I going to do? I didn't want to get into a fight with her, and hear my dad yell, "Whaddya wanna talk about that for?"

As I got older, I realized they most likely had given my dog away because they didn't want to pay for the upkeep. My *old* puppy Snoopy was a Lab and he might have ended up weighing a good 80 pounds and living for thirteen years. My parents made very little money and it was always poorly managed. That same year, 1967, we ate hot dogs and beans for Thanksgiving. A dog was just one more expense they wouldn't have to deal with. They had not thought it out when they said "yes" to letting me have him. But had they ever explained this to me and apologized? Never.

I accepted it the best I could. It was what it was. Although it puzzled me how my parents could be so unaware, so unconscious, of the intense trauma they created in their child's life. Just because it was no big deal to them, didn't mean it wasn't a big deal to me. Time to let it go and move on. Hanging on to *old stuff* is not healthy.

I had my new Snoopy. That's all that mattered. He took away the pain I had suffered in the past and made the future bright. Forgiving is tough, no matter how much time passes.

I visited my parents a few times a year and always brought Snoopy along. He made my dad more tolerable and brightened my mom's day. It was good to see her happy. She'd play with him and give him dog biscuits. Snoopy liked her. My dad was indifferent to him. Once in a while he'd call Snoopy to come to him, which he wouldn't do, until I gave the command of "Go on, Snoopy!" Then Snoopy would make his way over to him, and Dad would pet him.

Once Dad gave Snoopy a command to sit, and he wouldn't. So, Dad smacked Snoopy *really hard* on the rear, trying to get him to do it. When I saw this I yelled, "Don't hit him!" and I moved Snoopy away. Dad claimed he only "tapped" him. Some tap. How'd he like me to tap him in the face? When Mom passed away in 2000, I went to visit Dad and brought along Snoopy. Snoopy wandered through the apartment looking for her. He missed Mom too.

-15-

DOG PARKS

Before adopting Snoopy I didn't know what a dog park was. For all I knew it was a place where people parked their dogs while they went shopping. In a city like Los Angeles anything is possible. There you can find psychics for dogs, masseuses, chiropractors, psychiatrists, acupuncturists, orthodontists, even cosmetic plastic surgeons, and who knows what else?

I soon found out how much fun dog parks could be. When Snoopy's vaccination shots where complete, it was time to get him socialized with other dogs. I was still hanging around my group of friends with dogs. They regularly took their dogs to the Silver Lake Dog Park on Silver Lake Boulevard in Los Angeles. So that's where I decided to take Snoopy. It was several miles from my apartment. I didn't mind the drive, and I loved driving with Snoopy in my car.

He would always lie in the backseat. If I rolled down the rear windows, he would only look outside if a smell happened to catch his fancy. He wasn't one of those dogs who kept his head constantly out the window. Most of the time, he would chill-out in the backseat with a smile on his face as the wind rolled off his fur. He was cool that way. He was happy to be out with his master and go wherever the day took him. I wish I had the ability to be mellow like him and just go with the flow.

I was nervous the first time I took him to the dog park, and so was he. All these strange dogs of various shapes and sizes were everywhere; running, playing, hanging out with their owners. What if one of them attacked my dog? I would go berserk. I kept Snoopy on-leash the first few times. A few dogs came by to sniff, "hello," and it was fine.

After several visits he became acquainted with the space and I let him off-leash. He would play with a few dogs, usually ones close to his size. Bigger dogs, he stayed away from. Most of the time, he would stay within several yards of me.

Wanda had recently adopted a black-and-brown German Shepherd mix-breed puppy named Eddie, who was around Snoopy's age and size. Eddie had a wild energy about him and only three legs. One of his hind legs had been amputated because of an accident. No one was sure what kind of accident. Whether a car hit him, or if someone ran him over with a lawnmower. Another poor rescue dog with a shady background. Eddie was always a good conversation starter. This pup was quick, too. He ran as fast with three legs, if not faster, than most dogs of the four-legged variety. Eddie and Snoopy became fast friends. They enjoyed each other's company and would play until they wore each other out.

From time to time at the dog park fights would break out between dogs. I'd hear growling, barking, and teeth clacking. I'd scream, "Snooooopy!" hoping he wasn't being attacked, only to find him several yards away, every single time, watching the fighting dogs go at it until their owners broke it up. He was never near the action. It was as if he knew to stay out of harm's way, a sense he got right before a fight was going down.

Snoopy was quick for a dog his size, and sometimes his genetic agility, along with his smarts, would come in handy. Once I watched a large, full-grown Shepherd mix, weighing a good 70 pounds, aggressively chase after him. It was obvious Snoopy did not like this dog. Snoopy ran towards a large tree, with the big dog right on his tail. He got within inches of it, turned on a dime, and ran in another direction. The Shepherd mix plowed head-first into the tree. It instantly brought him to a full stop. The Shepherd mix stumbled away like he'd been hit in the face by a prize fighter who outclassed him by a couple of weight categories. He never chased Snoopy again. I called Snoopy over. I had a good laugh and praised him. He was a bit out of breath. I gave him some water and we went home.

Over the years of taking him to this dog park there were numerous fun incidents, as well as scary and boring ones.

One that comes to mind was when I took Snoopy there on a late morning. The park was almost empty, maybe one or two dogs running around with their owners nearby. A clean-cut white guy, about thirty, pulled curbside in front of the park in a faded, light-blue Ford F-150 pickup truck. In the back, standing on all fours, appeared to be a full-grown wolf.

The guy got out of the truck. The wolf jumped down and they entered the park through the gated entrance. This wolf was absolutely gorgeous. His coat was grey and white with a tinge of black throughout, and he had bright brown eyes.

I was fascinated by him and fearful at the same time. I'd never seen a wolf in the flesh. I looked for Snoopy to put him on-leash for safety sake, and I saw him running toward the wolf. My heart raced for a moment, but my panic turned to a smile as they both started running and playing together like kindred spirits. Snoopy, who was normally fearful and bothered by dogs much larger than himself, *loved* this wolf. I couldn't believe my eyes. Snoopy would nestle his head underneath the bigger dog's rib cage as if saying, "Hey, big guy, you're cool with me, I like you." The wolf seemed delighted by it. It was as if the wolf instantaneously became the Alpha male to Snoopy.

After Snoopy and the wolf had their playtime together, I went over and talked to the wolf's owner. I was scared to pet his wolf, but when he called him over it was obvious he was a gentle giant. I petted his soft, fluffy fur—a magnificent creature. He looked like he just walked down from the mountains, and he must have weighed at least 100 pounds. It was thrilling just to be standing next to him. No one in their right mind would mess with a guy with a wolf. Tough guys with Pit Bulls would back off.

I had heard of people having wolf-hybrids—half-wolf and half German Shepherd or Husky. At that time, under California law, you could have a fifty-fifty hybrid. I asked the owner how he got away with having a wolf as a pet. The guy told me he wasn't 100 percent; he was more like 75 percent wolf, 25 percent dog. But the paperwork he had for him said he was fifty-fifty, so he was legal. Who knew if he was telling the truth? The animal looked 100 percent. I didn't care. Whatever his wolf was, it was one awesome animal. Snoopy had a blast hanging with him, and I have a memory that still brings a smile to my face.

There were so many different types of dogs and people who came to the park. Two I remember well. A guy with a sweet Pit Bull, who wanted his dog to be tough and scary, and a lady with a rowdy Beagle. The guy, a tatted-up twenty-something Hispanic dude in a sleeveless tee-shirt, strolled in the park one day with his Pit Bull. The guy had his dog wearing a chain around its neck that looked like it was used to tow cars—it was thick. It was held together with a huge padlock. The dog looked ridiculous. Like a gangster rapper with really bad taste. The Pit Bull looked like he was embarrassed to wear it. You could tell the dog had a sweet demeanor, not a mean bone in its body.

The guy was yelling at him to chase after other dogs in the park, and he didn't want to. He just sniffed the ground and wandered around a tree. After several minutes of the Pit Bull not doing what he was told, the guy got frustrated, kicked the dog and took him out of the park.

When people like him would come around, no one would ever say anything. First off, this guy looked psycho. No one wanted to confront him. Who am I, or anyone else, to tell someone how to raise their dog? It would be like trying to tell someone how to raise their child.

The lady with the rowdy Beagle looked like a librarian with a kinky side. Her dog was *extremely* loud. This Beagle didn't weight more than fifteen pounds, but when its high-pitched bark came out of its mouth you needed ear plugs. It annoyed the other dogs as well, and Snoopy couldn't stand being anywhere near it. His sensitive ears must have been seriously hurting. The Beagle's bark was short and

repetitive, sounding like "*Arr-Arr-Arr-Arr-Arr-Arr-Arr.*"
He didn't howl, like most Beagles, just "*Arr-Arr-Arr-Arr-Arr-Arr-Arr.*" And it sounded like they were all blended together in a continuous loop for minutes at a time.

It was kind of funny to watch everyone's reactions to this loud, long-winded pooch, as he ran around in circles, barking. Of course no one wants to say anything. But I had to. Right when the Beagle was in the middle of an "*Arr-Arr-Arr-Arr-Arr-Arr-Arr,*" I pointed at it and yelled, "Somebody help the poor dog. He swallowed a car alarm!" Got a laugh.

We went to various dog parks over the years. There was Laurel Canyon Dog Park on Mulholland Drive near Laurel Canyon Boulevard, in Studio City, California. The park was hilly and muddy a lot of the time, and *waaaaay* too Hollywood for me. It seemed like many of the dog owners were actress-model types, carrying pocket pooches, a-la Paris Hilton. Either that or they were suburban guys with Pit Bulls trying to act tough and meet women. Not my cup of tea. Obviously, other types of people came to this park with their dogs, but it seemed like every time I went there with Snoopy we'd see those types. We went there a total of maybe six times.

I realized I didn't want to bring Snoopy there anymore when I watched an obnoxious twentyish, *model-actress-waitress*, also known as a *MAW*, in a tight dress and five-inch high heels *chase* after her dog while screaming its name in a posh-sounding voice. Her dog was the ugliest mutt I'd ever seen. It looked like a Pekingese-Sloth mix, and his name was Mango. Yes, Mango. Like the fruit. Plus, the way she called out his name, over and over again, stretching out the syllables..."Mang-Ooooo...Mang-Ooooo. Come here, Mang-Ooooo," was so annoying. The ugly mutt kept moving further and further away from her as she tried to keep her balance running in those ridiculous shoes. That was it, I was done. I couldn't take anymore. No more Laurel Canyon Dog Park for me. Of course Snoopy couldn't have cared less.

After a few years I got bored with taking him to dog parks. They no longer served their original purpose. Snoopy was well-socialized with other dogs. Several months after Snoopy passed away I drove by the Silver Lake Dog Park on my way to an appointment. As I looked over and saw people with their dogs a wave of memories hit me, and I started to cry. It was a hard, sad, lonely cry. It was a reminder of all the fun we'd had, and those precious times were gone.

-16-

CHICAGO, SILVER SQUIRRELS, SNOWBALLS, AND THE PIT BULL

In late December 1997, when Snoopy was roughly eight months old, I took him to Chicago on our first vacation together. It was pre-9/11, when it was fun to fly and airport security was safer. Less government control, no TSA lackeys frisking senior citizens, babies or disabled people, because according to their criteria, they might be terrorists. This was the only plane ride Snoopy ever went on. I hate to think what they do to dogs now. They probably get full body x-ray scans, shooting radiation into their bodies, along with canine cavity searches. I would never get a full body x-ray scan, let alone subject man's best friend to such an unnecessary invasion of privacy.

Several weeks before our travel adventure I purchased a medium-sized airline approved animal carrier. Snoopy didn't particularly like to be in a kennel, or a carrier, but he was a good boy and went along with it. In order to get him used to being in the carrier for an extended period of time, like on the plane, I placed it in the backseat of my car, put him in it, and drove him around the city. I did this for various stretches of time, often 45 minutes or more. The longest was two hours, on a drive to Palmdale, California and back, which was about an hour from Burbank.

I followed the airline rules and regulations regarding pet travel. At the Los Angeles International Airport terminal, they took the carrier with Snoopy in it from me, curbside, like he was a piece of check-in luggage. I found it very discomforting. Beforehand, I had taken him for a walk to pee and made sure he didn't drink too much water before the flight. I kissed him goodbye and told him I'd see him in a few hours. I was a bit paranoid from reading stories about dogs freezing to death in storage areas in the bowels of a plane, or dying for some unknown reason because of a plane ride. It wasn't like we were flying to sunny Hawaii or the Caribbean. We were both about to freeze our butts off for ten days in Chicago. But Snoopy had the advantage; he had a built-in fur coat.

Our flight had a two-hour layover and plane change in Minneapolis. I was able to see him during that time along with other pet folk on the plane who wanted to make sure their furry kids were okay. Snoopy saw me coming toward his carrier and let out a whining puppy cry of joy and relief. I can't imagine what was going through his brain. He probably had abandonment issues from his first owners, or whomever, and here I was putting him in a carrier, letting him fly through the air in the freezing cold in the bowels of a plane with other dogs in carriers, like a piece of luggage. One can only speculate about what air turbulence does to a dog's sensitive ears. I felt bad for him.

I took Snoopy out of the carrier and he jumped all over

me. I kissed and hugged him, then put him on-leash and took him outside to pee. After a few minutes I brought him back inside and stayed with him until an attendant told me it was time to put him back in the carrier. I told him everything would be okay and kissed him goodbye one more time. Thankfully, the flight back to Los Angeles was non-stop, so his time being uncomfortable would be lessened.

We arrived in Chicago and it was cold. An easy twenty degrees, and at times during our stay, it got down below zero. We stayed with Dottie and Jack, the parents of my former roommate; a well-known clairvoyant to the stars. They lived in a section of town called Rogers Park. Not only were they kind enough to let me stay with them for ten days for the holidays, but they allowed me to bring Snoopy.

They lived in a modest two-story brick house built in the late 1800s. Dottie and Jack, both in their seventies, enjoyed Snoopy's puppy energy. It was like having a little kid with four feet running through their house.

Jack, a lifelong Chicagoan, was a retired regional safety director for Coca-Cola, who loved eating chocolate-covered cherries, gardening, betting against the Chicago Cubs, and making fun of the Pope. Dottie, his better half, was a former secretary, who had raised eight kids and had a wicked sense of humor. She once played a birthing film for a group of neighborhood children in reverse.

Snoopy adapted nicely to these temporary surroundings. He followed me everywhere I went, well...like a puppy. What a joyous feeling. He slept at the foot of my bed in the upstairs bedroom where I camped out.

I would walk Snoopy two or three times a day. I hadn't seen ice and snow on the ground like that since I was a kid in Detroit. It would have been fun to have Snoopy pull me along the ice covered sidewalk like Bushy had, but he was too small...and I was too big. Living in California for so many years, I was now a bit of a crybaby when it came to cold climates, and the Windy City was a cold one, especially in December. There was one thing I forgot about the Midwest...silver squirrels. They were everywhere in the neighborhood, and Snoopy *loved* to chase squirrels.

Every time I took him for a walk it seemed like there was one or two of these silver squirrels every fifty feet. They were slightly furry, silver-grey in color, and about a foot and a half long, including a fuzzy tail. Snoopy would whine whenever he'd see one and try to chase after them, as they high-tailed it for the nearest tree or bush. He'd try to climb up the trees to get to them, his front paws scratching at the tree bark. I'd have to hold his leash tighter than usual. A few times it felt like he was going to pull my arm out of its socket as he tried to get at one of these rat descendants.

He didn't want to hurt them; he wanted to sniff them and get them to play. Snoopy was curious about most animals, and if he saw one out and about, well, maybe he'd make a new friend. The difficult part about walking him near these silver squirrels was that he was so hyped-up when he saw them, he would not take a dump. For some unknown reason, he refused to poop when he would see and smell silver squirrels.

I would have to walk quite a distance to a non-residential area with no trees, or find a parking lot, in order to get him to poop. I was not a happy bunny. I was freezing my tail off and he was having the time of his life. Sure, the first couple of times it was fun. I got a thrill out of watching him be so happy. But when it started to drop below zero—the heck with silver squirrels. At least they weren't as meaningless as street pigeons, which seem to exist for no other reason than to wreck the paint on your car by crapping on it.

Playing in the snow with my pup was more fun than words can describe. Snoopy's Sheltie ancestors were from Scotland, where it gets very cold. He was made for the snow. This was his first time being in it and he absolutely loved it. We'd play in Dottie and Jack's snow covered backyard. I rolled around in it and made snow angels. Snoopy rolled around in it too.

For those of you who haven't lived in a snowy region of the world. A snow angel is made when you lie on your back on an undisturbed area of fresh snow, like on a lawn, with your legs straight and your arms at your sides. You then move your arms and legs as if you were doing jumping jacks. The imprint this leaves in the snow is like that of a winged human or angel, hence, snow angel. I tried teaching Snoopy how to make one, but he couldn't get the hang of it.

Another fun thing I would do is make a snowball, show it to Snoopy and yell "Get the ball!" and throw it. He'd run after it. The snowball would blend in with the fallen snow and he could never find it. He'd look in the direction of where it landed, put his cute snout in the snow to try and grab it, and come up with nothing. He'd look around like, "What the heck?" and I would fall over from laughing so hard. I did this several times until I was laughed out. Regretfully, there weren't any cell phones with video cameras in 1997, or I would've had a great piece of video. If there had been YouTube, that video would have gone viral.

Dottie and Jack were fun to hang out with. Not like

my parents, who I couldn't spend more than a few hours with before I felt like pulling my hair out of my head. Their house had a warm family atmosphere I wished I'd had as a kid. But...talk to their kids and they might have felt about Dottie and Jack the way I did about my parents. It's like that sometimes. Your friends found your parents warm and understanding, and vice versa. Or maybe you had loving, supportive parents to guide you through various stages of life, even the difficult teenage years, without so much as an argument or disagreement. And maybe you're from Jupiter or Middle Earth.

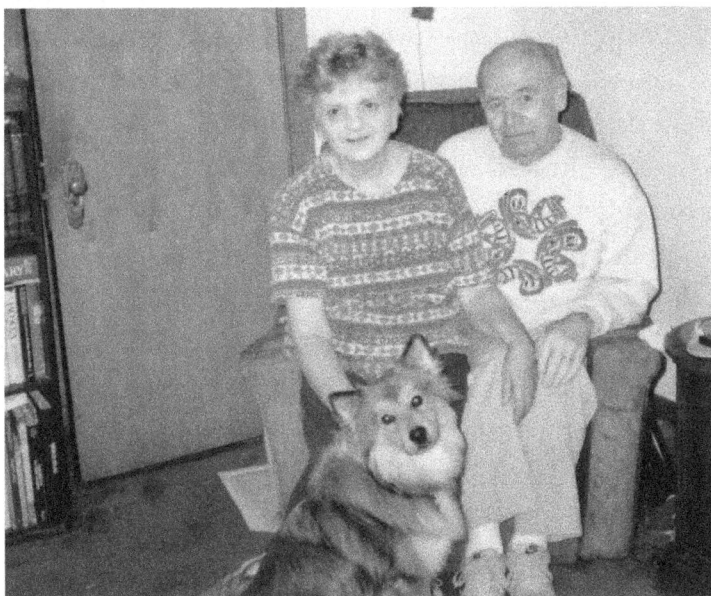

Dottie and Jack posing with Snoopy

Anyhow, I very much liked Dottie and Jack. Dottie was one of the funniest people I've ever met. She made me laugh harder than many of the well-known stand-up comedians I worked with. It was just her demeanor, along with her thick

Chicago accent, dry sense of humor, and sarcastic outlook. She had me keeling over with laughter on several occasions.

There is one Dottie story I must share. A cousin on her husband Jack's side of the family, who she didn't like, gave birth to a pair of conjoined twins, joined at the head. It was big news in Chicago. Conjoined twins are considered a rare phenomenon. The twins' pictures were on the front page of the local newspapers. Dottie was invited to their baby shower which she didn't particularly want to go to, but went out of respect for her husband. Beforehand, she called her children into the kitchen, showed them the pictures in the newspapers and in a sincere tone with that thick Chicago accent said, "Okay, kids, we're going to go to your cousins' baby shower and we need to get 'em gifts. Now, remember: no hats and no pullover sweaters." That's funny!

Back to our visit with Dottie and Jack. When I would go out to explore the great city of Chicago in my rental car and "play tourist," I left Snoopy with them. They were pretty much homebodies, so it was perfect. I'd kiss him goodbye and go about my day, sometimes being gone for eight or nine hours. Jack told me Snoopy would never move from his new-found resting spot next to the front door I exited out of, not even to get a drink of water. He and Dottie would call him, but he wouldn't come. He stayed at the front door with a sad puppy face waiting for his master to return. Loyalty a human could never comprehend.

One morning, before my walk with Snoopy, Dottie asked me to take some Christmas cookies she'd made to her next-door neighbor. No problem. I would deliver the cookies and then Snoopy and I would go on our walk. I headed outside in my winter garb with an aluminum foil covered cookie dish in one hand, and Snoopy's leash in the other. Snoopy raised his nose and his nostrils dilated to get a better whiff of the cookies as we headed up the steps to the neighbor's house.

I rang the doorbell. A few seconds passed and a kindly gentleman in his sixties answered and gave me a look like, "What are you and your dog doing at my front door?" I introduced myself and Snoopy. Told him we were staying next door with Dottie and Jack for the holidays, that we were visiting from California, and that Dottie asked me to bring him some Christmas cookies she'd made. He looked at the aluminum foil covered cookie dish in my hand and smiled.

I don't remember his name, but what sticks out vividly in my mind is what happened when he opened the front screen door and took the cookie dish. In what seemed like less than a second, a full-grown, scary-looking Pit Bull ran out of the house, around the screen door and came right at Snoopy. *I freaked out.*

I started screaming, "Help! Help! Get it away! Get it away!" among my dozens of cuss words. I grabbed Snoopy's leash and pulled him up onto his hind legs, trying to get him away from this dog, and practically choking him in the process. The scary-looking Pit Bull was growling and I heard his upper teeth repeatedly hit his lower teeth as he snapped at Snoopy like some kind of ticked-off giant snapping turtle. The gentleman quickly ran onto the porch, grabbed the scary-looking Pit Bull by his collar, and dragged him back into the house. My heart was pounding. I almost wet my pants.

I lowered Snoopy back down to the porch. He was

gagging from the strain his collar put on his throat when I pulled him up. The gentleman and now his wife both came onto the porch to apologize. Normally, I would have told them both where to go and reported them and their vicious beast to animal control. But I was staying next-door as a guest and it seemed no one was hurt. I was as polite as I could be under the circumstances.

It turns out the scary-looking Pit Bull wasn't trying to hurt Snoopy; he was simply letting him know this was *his* turf. He didn't bite Snoopy, or me. His owners told me the scary-looking Pit Bull had never seen another dog on the porch before, and he *reacted.* I later found out that everyone in the neighborhood who owned a dog knew not to go near their house. Then I was told this couple had *another* Pit Bull they kept in their garage, who was considered *the mean one.* It had attacked a mailman—twice. The one Snoopy and I encountered was the nicer of the two. Holy moly! Then I thought about what occurred. The scary-looking Pit Bull *didn't bark* when I rang the doorbell, like most dogs. What a sneaky dog. I do not trust Pit Bulls. I really wish I would have known about those dogs. I would have never taken Snoopy over there. Poor baby.

The scary-looking Pit Bull's owners came over to visit Dottie and Jack later that evening. Again they apologized to me. I think they really stopped by to make sure Snoopy was okay, and thankfully he was. On the flip side, I have seen some sweet, loving Pit Bulls over the years. I assume it's how you raise them. Overall our trip to Chicago was great fun, except for the scare with the scary-looking Pit Bull.

-17-

SEPARATION ANXIETY AND FRIED TORTILLA CHIPS

A few weeks after our trip to Chicago, I had a stand-up comedy gig in Modesto, California, a one-nighter. Modesto is located in the central valley area of *Northern California*. This was not a good gig, but I didn't want to cancel on Don, the booker, who was a friend. You usually couldn't trust the people who booked these little one-night gigs as far as you could throw them, but Don was a good guy. There was a nervous energy about Don. He reminded me of a high school gym teacher who was frustrated that he never became a pro athlete.

My friend, Virginia, a former Playboy bunny, known as Bunny Ginger, who spent the last twenty years as a music editor for the movies, loved Snoopy. I asked if she wouldn't mind watching him for a couple of days. The answer was an exuberant "yes." This was the first time I'd had to leave him for more than eight or ten hours. I assumed he would be okay. I assumed *I* would be okay. What's two days? Actually, less than two days. It was a five-hour drive north. I planned on driving up Saturday morning, doing the gig Saturday night, driving back Sunday morning, and arriving home late Sunday afternoon. I dropped Snoopy off at Virginia's apartment with his leash and collar, dog food, doggie treats, water bowl, and a few of his favorite toys.

I kissed him goodbye, told him to be a good boy, and that I would see him in a couple of days. Not that he understood what I said, but I would like to think he did on some level. I considered him to be like a person. A person you'd want to be around all day, every day. Being away from him for less than a couple of days didn't seem like it would be a big deal.

Snoopy's "don't leave me" face

I got to Modesto late Saturday afternoon. I drove directly to Don's house. I was spending the night there after the gig. I called Virginia to check on Snoopy. She said he was doing fine. I went to the gig in the early evening. It was at a Mexican restaurant. They had a 200-seat room in the back with a makeshift stage, microphone, and sound system. Not bad for this type of low-end gig.

Before the show I was offered a free dinner and drinks. I didn't drink and I was a hard-core vegan. I declined the food. It was an upscale Mexican restaurant with authentic Mexican food, which meant, more than likely, they used lard in many of their dishes. I wasn't taking any chances. I would eat later, someplace else. Don suggested I eat some chips and salsa. There couldn't be any lard in them, especially the salsa.

I called over a waiter to make sure. I asked him if the chips were cooked in lard. He said they weren't...so I placed an order. He left for a few minutes then returned with a basket of warm, salty, freshly-made tortilla chips and a bowl of fresh salsa. He placed them in front of me. I thanked him, and he left. I grabbed a couple chips and popped them into my mouth. They tasted good, *real good*. They were so good I couldn't stop eating them. I started to worry why they tasted so good. The owner of the restaurant saw Don and me eating, and stopped by our table. I was introduced as the headlining act from Los Angeles for the night's show. He seemed like a pleasant guy.

Suddenly, I started to get more paranoid about the chips. I'm neurotic to begin with, and I was really into veganism. No eating of any animal products for me whatsoever. I complimented the owner on the chips and salsa, and politely asked if the chips were cooked in lard. He smiled proudly and said, "Yes. Delicious, aren't they?" Oh, no! Oh, no! Oh, no! I started to gag. I jumped up from my seat and without saying a word to anyone, ran for the men's room.

As I was running, I heard Don telling the owner that I had a slight case of diarrhea, but I'd be okay for the show. I made my way into the men's room, went to the sink and looked in the mirror. I was completely pale. I ran the cold water and splashed my face several times. I rested two fingers inside my mouth and contemplated sticking them down my throat, to puke up the chips in my stomach. I couldn't. I was too big of a baby. I'd thrown up before, and it wasn't pretty.

Don entered the men's room to make sure I was okay. I went into a rant about my diet and the careless waiter, who didn't know how the chips were cooked. To calm myself, I had Don go to a convenience store down the street and buy me a two-liter bottle of purified water. I guzzled it down, hoping I could flush the lard out of my body, sooner rather than later. I quickly realized I was just going to have to chill-out and let nature take its course. Don begged me not to badmouth the restaurant from the stage; he had to come back for future shows. I promised I wouldn't, and I didn't. The show was a success. I did my required 45-minute set, got my fix of laughs from the audience, and we headed back to his house. Don's wife, Joyce, made me a big veggie salad, which made me feel a lot better.

We all watched a little TV, then I headed into the back bedroom where I was spending the night, and crashed on the bed. I was tired from the drive up, the show, and the stress of eating lard-fried tortilla chips. I looked up at the ceiling, my hands cupped behind my head. I began to think about Snoopy and how much I missed him.

I felt a wave of weariness slowly engulf my body. I started to breathe heavier than normal. I began shaking and hyperventilating for several minutes. I had a burning desire to get in the car *right now* and drive back to get Snoopy, but I was way too tired. I calmed down my breathing and called Virginia to check on him.

She said that he was okay, except he would not eat his food. That was odd. Snoopy normally scarfed down his bowl of dry food within a minute. Plus, she said he spent most of his time lying at her front door. We both missed each other. I suppose this might be called separation anxiety.

It was never that bad again when I went away. But the first time was a doozy. We both got used to it. When I picked him up Sunday, in the late afternoon, Virginia said his appetite improved, he ate all his food that morning, and he didn't stay by the front door as much. He knew I was coming home soon.

Virginia enjoyed her time with Snoopy so much that whenever she could, she took care of him when I went out of town. She did it for nine years. She became his "Aunt Virginia" and she and Snoopy built wonderful memories together.

-18-

WENDY

Snoopy and I had been together about a year when I started to date again. I had dated sporadically for a few years but hadn't had a serious relationship in quite a while.

With Snoopy in my life I felt like I was becoming more of a loving person. He was bringing out a nurturing side of me I really hadn't experienced before. I had always been a bit self absorbed, but I lost some of that when I took on the responsibility of caring for him. Performers, actors, entertainers, and the like seem very prone to being egocentric. I guess it sometimes goes along with being the center of attention in one's work. They're all about *mi-mi-mi-mi*. Snoopy was helping me get out of *mi-mi-mi-mi*, which allowed me to share my new feelings with a significant other.

Wendy, a pretty, petite, hazel-eyed young lady I had dated the year before, but lost touch with, had been on my mind. We had a lot in common—from similar points of view on healthy eating and exercise, to politics, and on and on. I was in a different place, so I decided to call her. Luckily she still had the same phone number, and fortunately for me she wasn't seeing anyone. We started to date again and have been together ever since.

A dog lover, Wendy fell instantly in love with Snoopy, kind of like I did. She became his new so-called "mom." I know this is going to sound strange, weird, or wacky, or whatever, and it's not my imagination because Wendy is my witness. Snoopy became jealous of the time I spent with her when we were first going out.

He had been the main focus of my attention. When Wendy came along, he stayed home alone more than usual. Maybe it's the same type of reaction a childless couple with a dog has when a newborn baby comes into their lives and their pooch takes a backseat to their time and affection. I remember one incident in particular that showed me Snoopy was truly jealous of Wendy.

One evening Wendy and I were cuddling on the couch. Snoopy was resting in his favorite spot by the picture window. I called him, "Snoopy, come here. Here, Snoopy!" He wouldn't come. This was odd. My well-behaved, obedient dog was disobeying? I called him again, but louder, "Snoopy, come here! Here, Snoopy!" No response. I went over to see what was wrong. He had a long face, as if he were moping. I said, "What's wrong?" He looked at me with sad eyes.

Wendy came over. He looked at her and made a sort of disappointed sound. It wasn't a growl. It was more of a disappointed sigh that said, "What are *you* doing here? Can't you leave me alone with my master?" Then he made another disappointed sound and this time he turned away from her as if he were saying, "Please just go." We both immediately sensed what he was communicating. We laughed because it was so strange...and adorably cute. I turned to Wendy and said, "He's jealous of you." She let out a sympathetic, "Oh, Snoopy." We hugged him and reassured him everything would be okay. He seemed to know what we meant. I gave him a biscuit. Wendy gave him an extra one. He was now more of a happy camper. Slowly, but surely, Snoopy accepted Wendy and they became great friends for the rest of his life.

Snoopy, me and Wendy in our first family photo

-19-

MELVIN THE CAT

Wendy and I had been dating about ten months when she decided to adopt a kitten. First she went to one of the many cat rescues in Los Angeles. She found a beautiful eight week-old, male, gray kitten she liked and was interviewed by the woman who ran the place. Actually, it was more like an interrogation—wanting to know *everything* about Wendy—as if she were applying for a million-dollar loan with no collateral.

The cat rescue woman was a bit of nutcase. One of these people who'd rather keep the cats and kittens she had rescued for herself than adopt them out. After the interrogation, Wendy was allowed to take the gray kitten home...for a trial period. The cat rescue woman would then have to inspect and approve Wendy's apartment, to make sure it was a suitable living space. Wendy lived in a small studio apartment, located in the Los Feliz area of Los Angeles. It was an older remodeled building, probably 1950s, made of wood, stucco, and very little brick.

I brought Snoopy over to see if he and the gray kitten would get along. He hadn't been around many cats or kittens, but the ones he had, he always wanted to play with them, whether they wanted to or not. The gray kitten took one look at Snoopy and almost crapped a kitten brick. He hissed as loud as he could, raised his little front paws with his claws out, and then ran under the bed. He probably would have scratched Snoopy's face, if I had not had him on-leash. Not a good sign.

I also had to look at it from the gray kitten's point of view. We had no idea of his background. He could have been terrified by a dog at some point in his short life. Snoopy must have seemed like a towering monster with big fangs to the little fella. Wendy calmed down the gray kitten the best she could. I left with Snoopy. We'd deal with it at a later time.

That time never came. The cat rescue woman came over to Wendy's place and decided it was unsuitable. She saw a small vent in the wall with a painted metal covering, and was scared the kitten might somehow remove it, crawl into the vent, and get hurt, or trapped. As if the kitten knew how to use a screwdriver. The cat rescue woman was looking for any excuse not to give up the kitten. Plus, the contract Wendy would have had to sign had all sorts of stipulations, like having the cat rescue woman check up on the kitten every few months, turning in veterinarian reports, all kinds of stuff. Though Wendy was disappointed, she got over it. I suggested she get a kitten where I got Snoopy, the Burbank Animal Shelter.

That weekend we went to the shelter. The Cat and Kitten section was much smaller than the dog area. It was located in a separate room behind the dogs. The cats and kittens available for adoption were various sizes and colors and they ranged in age from eight weeks to seniors.

I wasn't always a fan of cats. My mother was terrified of cats. I was ten the first time I saw this happen, the same year I was given my first Snoopy puppy. One afternoon a full-grown cat from the neighborhood was resting on the outside windowsill of the large picture window in our living room. I saw him, or her, at the same time my mom did. Mom starting screaming like it was a wild panther that was going to jump through the window and kill her. The cat stayed on the windowsill watching her scream, like it didn't have a care in the world. Mom then started yelling for me to, "Get it away! Get it away!" I went outside and shooed it off the windowsill. It jumped down onto the front porch and took off running.

This experience didn't sit well with me. I don't remember seeing many cats at that point in my life, and no one I knew had cats. The one time I heard someone mention cats was couple of years earlier, when I was eight. In my old neighborhood, some older bad boys, around eleven or twelve, were blowing off firecrackers in the alley, which I thought was cool. They wanted me to go hunt down cats with them and blow some off—*in the cats' butts*. They were not joking.

These Detroit boys were a different breed. They were wild and they scared me. One of them pulled my arm for me to come along with them. I pulled away and ran...like the cat, who had run off the windowsill.

After these experiences I was indifferent to cats. After all, if Mom didn't like them and others wanted to hurt them, there must me something wrong with them, right? I had that going-on psychologically about cats as an adult.

Throughout the years I had dated women and had friends who had cats. My attitude slowly changed about them and I began to see them as mysterious creatures of beauty. It also seemed I had some sort of allergic reaction to them. If I was in a room with a cat for more than a couple hours my eyes would slightly water and my throat would get itchy. I was told by a doctor that I might be allergic to cat dander. Somehow, in time, I overcame this by being around the kitten Wendy was about to adopt.

As Wendy and I looked at the caged cats and kittens up for adoption I found it more pleasurable than looking at the dogs. It seemed more of the dogs were on their last legs and about to be euthanized. It looked like doggie death row, only they had done nothing wrong. So sad. When you walked by some would give you those sad dog eyes that said "help me" and you knew you couldn't.

There were a few cats hanging-on to the last days of their lives, but most were adoptable. I was drawn to a rambunctious kitten with white and marble coloring. Wendy didn't like him. At first I kept insisting she get him; he was too awesome not to adopt. I had an attendant take him out of his cage so we could play with him. Wendy still didn't want him, too wild for her. Finally, I shut my mouth and put aside my controlling attitude. This was going to be her cat, and her responsibility, so the decision should be hers and hers alone.

Wendy noticed two medium-haired, black-and-white kitten siblings in a cage off to the right side of the room, both very pretty. One sat in front of the cage looking out, and the other lay quietly in back. The one in front hissed at Wendy. Hearing that, I moved along to the other cages.

Wendy told the attendant to take out the kitten *behind* the hissing kitten so she could get acquainted with him. She held him. He was adorable. More white than black, with a black spot on his white belly. I don't know why they always call cats or kittens that are black and white, *black-and-whites*, no matter how much white they have in them. Shouldn't some be called *white-and-blacks*? Plus, the term "black-and-white" sounds too much like a police car.

Anyhow, Wendy fell in love with this four month-old, pink-nosed, male black-and-white kitten, or white-and-black kitten, if you will. The date on the slip of paper clipped to the cage with his intake information indicated he was available to be adopted at anytime. Wendy took the slip to the counter at the front of the building, filled out the necessary paperwork, paid the fees, and adopted him. She named him...Melvin.

I had brought along an animal carrier, designed for cats or small dogs, and placed him in it. We stopped off at my apartment first, so Melvin could meet Snoopy before taking the new kitten to Wendy's place. We hoped they would get along better than Snoopy and the gray kitten.

Snoopy was excited to see me as usual, and he was definitely excited to see who, or what, was in the carrier I was holding. He whined with anticipation as I placed it on the coffee table in the living room, and opened the criss-cross metal door of the carrier. Melvin made no noise as he ventured out. He slowly put one front leg out, then the other, then his head. He wasn't scared of Snoopy one iota, nada, nothing...no fear whatsoever. They touched nose-to-nose as if to say "hello." Melvin then walked completely out of the carrier. Snoopy sniffed him all over. Melvin couldn't have cared less, and Snoopy's size wasn't a problem. He was cool with it, and so were we. We had just introduced Snoopy to his new best friend for life.

What were the odds of adopting a kitten from a shelter, not

knowing any of its background, and having it not be scared of a dog much larger than himself? We simply lucked out.

There was no contact name listed on Melvin's intake information. The people at the shelter had said Melvin and his brother were part of a litter dropped off anonymously in one of the cages in front of the building. The Burbank Animal Shelter had a few permanent outside cages were people could drop off animals on their off hours. People have all sorts of reasons for placing animals up for adoption; some good, some bad. Whatever their reasons, the shelter allowed them to do it any hour of the day, thus giving many animals a new lease on life.

Melvin adjusted pretty quickly to Wendy's apartment and his new life with her, Snoopy, and me. One thing he learned to do in his new environment was to eat fast, and eat all his food at once. He learned this behavior because of Snoopy. Whenever Snoopy and I would come to visit, it was a real challenge trying to get him *not* to eat Melvin's food.

Melvin was too small at this point to be fed on a counter or cabinet, he couldn't jump that high. He had to be fed on the floor. Snoopy loved cat food as much as dog food. At first, he wouldn't eat Melvin's food if I was watching. He wasn't as overt about it, like he had been with Adelaide the Cocker Spaniel when he was a pup. However, when we spent the night and I'd fall asleep, Snoopy would quietly gobble down whatever was left of Melvin's food in the middle of the night.

I'd wake up in the morning and Melvin's food bowl would be licked clean. Of course Melvin couldn't say anything. He couldn't scream, "Hey, Snoopy! Leave my food alone. I like to eat slowly and when *I* feel like it. I'm a cat, for crying out loud!" Melvin did the best he could, but from then on whenever he was fed, he would scarf it all down as fast as he could. Whether it was out of fear of Snoopy eating his food, or merely imitating Snoopy—I don't know. Their nicknames became "Pig Dog" and "Pig Cat"—two cute furry boys who ate like pigs.

These boys had fun playing over the years. Snoopy played with Melvin as though he were playing with a dog buddy. During one playtime incident, when Melvin was still a kitten, I watched as Snoopy pranced around like a pony, jumped about a foot into the air and landed both of his front legs with all his upper body weight, on Melvin's back. It was like a wrestling move. Melvin was smashed down on the wood floor with all four legs spread-eagle. It scared me. Snoopy could have hurt little Melvin. But Melvin wasn't hurt, or fazed by it. He stood up, turned around and flung his paw at Snoopy, like a MMA fighter making a left hook. It's how they played.

Snoopy and Melvin waiting to be fed

Melvin's personality isn't like other cats I have been acquainted with, or like you see on television or in the movies...the ones who lovingly purr and lie in your lap for hours, or lie with you in bed all night long. Melvin isn't the most friendly or loving boy.

The most affection he shows is when he wants to be fed at mealtime, or when he wants more to eat, almost like a dog begging for food. Then he'll come over and say "hi" with a wisp of his body against your legs. He does surprise us every now and then and show affection by purring, wanting to be petted, or scratched under his chin. I rather like his aloof personality. He does things his way, and could not care less what anyone thinks. I wouldn't want a cat that lies on my lap all the time, or meows constantly, needing attention. I wouldn't get any work done. Melvin merely has eccentric ways, like most domestic felines.

He's also very cooperative when Wendy grooms him. He'll let her comb out his fur and cut his nails, no problem. He seems to enjoy it. I always tease him whenever he gets his nails cut. I blurt out, "Melvin's getting his nails done—like a girl." He usually gives me a look of "shut up." All in all, Melvin is a cool cat.

-20-

HIKING IN GRIFFITH PARK

Wendy's apartment was on Los Feliz Boulevard, about a third of a mile from a series of hiking trails in Griffith Park. When Snoopy and I would visit, we'd go hiking. Griffith Park is a landmark in Los Angeles, famous for their Observatory which was featured in the classic 1955 film about misunderstood youth, *Rebel Without a Cause*, starring James Dean and Natalie Wood. According to their website it is the largest municipal park with urban wilderness area in the United States—roughly 4,210 acres.

That's all fine and dandy, but I only found it interesting when I took Snoopy on the trails. Watching him run and play, and smell the woody smells, was utter joy. After a hike he'd pant from being tired, his tongue hanging out and a smile on his face. I'd give him a drink from my water bottle, which I always carried with me. His two front legs, which looked like was wearing a pair of furry white socks, would get dusty with dirt and end up looking like a pair of furry brown socks.

We'd hit the trails a few times a week. Occasionally, Wendy would come along. The trails were a way for me to relax and be in nature. Plus, it was good exercise for both of us. There were various lengths of trails. You could go on a half-mile hike, or a ten-mile one. Griffith Park was so massive you could hike all day if you wanted to. I stuck to the short trails I knew. It was very easy to get lost and end up at the Los Angeles Zoo, which was adjacent to the park, or along a stretch of road meant only for cars. It was best to not stray too far from home.

The first time I took Snoopy hiking there it was as though I was taking a six year old kid to Disneyland for the first time. He was overwhelmed. His nose most likely had never smelled that many smells in one location. From the dirt, to other dogs, to pine trees, to coyotes, to snakes in the brush, to homeless people hiding and camping out, to who knows what? There was never a time he didn't enjoy our outings on the trails of Griffith Park.

My beautiful boy loved the outdoors

There were a couple unnerving incidents, though. Once after we finished our hike and were on our way back down

Commonwealth Avenue, to Wendy's place, a Korean man was walking toward us with his beautiful, snow-white Chow Chow on-leash. I'm not a fan of the Chow Chow temperament. They can be snippy, moody, and downright nasty. I cautiously proceeded toward them, holding Snoopy several feet away. Snoopy was tired from his hike, but still excited to see the Chow Chow. I asked the owner, "Is he friendly with other dogs?" With a confident voice he said, "Oh, yeah." I lightened up on Snoopy's leash, and he approached the Chow Chow nose-to-nose.

They sniffed each other for several seconds, getting a sense of one another, tails wagging. Snoopy's ears perked up and he became totally animated. The Chow Chow kind-of danced in place for a moment like a dancing baby bear. I thought, "How cute is that?" Then in a split second the beautiful Chow Chow turned into a demon dog. His eyes widened slightly and I heard his teeth click together as his jaws ate air, and he tried to bite Snoopy. I immediately pulled Snoopy back and screamed at the owner, "You liar! Get your dog away from here!" Plus a few other choice words I won't repeat. The owner pulled his Chow Chow away, as it continuously barked and growled at Snoopy. Snoopy wasn't fazed at all. To him it was no big deal. Within seconds he was smiling, as we continued on our way back to Wendy's place. If only I could be like him in stressful situations.

From then on, if a dog looking anything remotely like a Chow Chow came near Snoopy, I moved him in the opposite direction. By no means are *all* Chow Chows bad, just like all politicians don't have horns and tails, but I wasn't taking any chances.

Then there was the time I saw two coyotes casually

walking along a trail, like they were dogs out for a stroll without their owners. Snoopy and I were on another trail and luckily I had him on-leash. He started to whine. It was the type of whine he made when he saw another dog and was anxious to play with him or her.

I looked around. I didn't see any dogs in front or in back of us. Snoopy started to move to my right. He normally walked to my left. He continued whining and moved towards an embankment, about ten feet to my right. I looked down the embankment. About thirty feet below us was another trail. Nonchalantly strolling along were two grayish-brown coyotes, both bigger than Snoopy. Snoopy saw them and started whining even louder. They looked up at us, and I pulled Snoopy out of their line of sight.

I wasn't certain if they were on the hunt for dog pray, but there they were, big as life, and I wasn't going to let them anywhere near my boy. I pulled Snoopy further away and to my left. I then started screaming, "Get! Get outta here!" at the top of my lungs, which I must admit is pretty darn loud. The coyotes took off running. I remembered reading that they were skittish around humans. I walked Snoopy out of the park as fast as I could.

That incident put me on my guard from then on while hiking with Snoopy in Griffith Park. I had heard too many stories about coyotes coming down from the hills of Los Angeles, snatching up cats and little dogs for food, and the howls of the coyotes mixed with the death cries of cats and dogs echoing in the night. I'm for helping animals, and adopting them from shelters, but I would have no problem fighting off a wild coyote out for the blood of my, or someone else's, beloved pet.

Overall, Griffith Park was a fun experience. The semi-fresh air and the beautiful views of the surrounding cities seen from different locations throughout the park, made it worthwhile. But most importantly, Snoopy absolutely loved being there.

Various companies would promote their services to dog owners at the park. One dog training service was very inventive. Whether or not they came up with the initial idea, I don't know. They had a one-day snake safety class for dogs. Griffith Park had snakes living and crawling around at various times of the year, and some were poisonous. Thankfully I'd never seen any while walking Snoopy. But I'd heard from other hikers about dogs getting bitten while out on the trails.

The snake safety class was simple. They would place *defanged* snakes along trails and in various areas where the dogs in the class could see them. Dogs, being curious creatures would approach the snakes to try and get a better look. The dog owners were pretty much guaranteed that the snakes would try to take a bite out of their dog. The snakes would lash out at the unsuspecting dog, and attempt to bite them with their toothless jaws. The dog now had the experience of getting attacked and *gummed* by this strange moving stick, and it scared the bejesus out of them. Hence, if they ever came across a normal snake while on the trails, or anywhere else, they'd stay away. A clever behavior modification trick.

-21-

EMILY AND LADY
AND THE TRAMP

I saw much more of my neighbor, Claudia, who worked at the Burbank Animal Shelter and had drawn the ticket that made Snoopy mine. In my eyes, she could do no wrong. Claudia owned two adopted dogs and a couple of cats from the shelter. One dog was a Pit Bull-Doberman Pinscher mix named Emily.

At first glance, if you saw Emily, you'd think she was a scary-looking 60 pound walking muscle. But she was so sweet, and full of play, to everyone who came close—you quickly got over *your fear*. If you petted Emily, within a few seconds, she'd roll over on her back for a tummy rub.

Emily had a great story. Claudia had received her at the shelter as a three week old puppy, starved almost to the point of being skin and bones. Since she was so far gone, others on staff felt the humane thing to do was euthanize her. Claudia saw the spark in Emily's eyes, took her home, and nursed her back to health. Instead of bringing her back to the shelter to be put up for adoption, Claudia decided to keep her.

Snoopy and Emily became pals for a few years, until she and Claudia moved away. They would play off-leash in the grass courtyard in front of the apartment building where they lived. Snoopy and Emily were about the same size, except Emily outweighed Snoopy by at least twenty pounds and those twenty pounds were solid muscle. She did not know her own strength. Once, while playing, they ran toward each other and hit chest-*to*-chest. Snoopy was hit with such force he stumbled back a several feet and hit the ground with a look on his face like, "What the heck was that?" He was used to playing with dogs his size, but never one with such power.

Claudia and I started laughing. She pulled Emily aside and I comforted Snoopy with a smile on my face. Poor baby; he had no idea his girlfriend could kick serious butt if she needed to.

Claudia had a teenage son, who liked to walk Emily through the neighborhood at lunchtime to watch the reactions of people on their way to eat at the nearby restaurants. The majority of the time people would see Emily approaching and they would walk into the street to avoid her then back onto the sidewalk when she was several yards away. Or they would walk across the street to avoid her entirely. Little did they know that in Emily's case looks were very deceiving.

Claudia invited Snoopy and me to an outdoor screening of the animated classic, *Lady and the Tramp* and we heartily accepted. She had received an extra ticket from the dog agility group Emily belonged to. Disney Studios in Burbank was having a DVD release party. People could bring their dogs and watch the movie on a huge outdoor screen while sitting on a couch with their pooch. It was being held on large parcel of grassy land adjacent to the studio. Snoopy and I arrived in the early evening. It was simply fantastic. There must have been at least 100 couches set up, along with all kinds of doggy-human activities. From agility tests, to dog food booths, to getting your dog's paw print in a piece of clay you could take home as a keepsake.

I attempted to get Snoopy in as many activities as I could before the sun went down and it was time to watch the movie. The atmosphere was blissful; men, women, and children with their dogs, having fun. Although, it was set-up mostly for dog activities, the humans were having fun too. Dogs don't need anything *set-up* for them to have fun. They can find joy and happiness in any activity.

At least that was my experience with Snoopy. The wind on his nose, or lying near my feet was enough to put a smile on his face. Maybe dogs don't smile, I'm not certain. But it sure seemed that way to me. He smiled quite a bit. He was a happy dog.

The folks at Disney had set-up a booth where you could sit at a table with your dog and they would take your picture. When they handed it to you, superimposed in the background were Lady and the Tramp in the spaghetti dinner scene from the movie, and it appeared as if you and your dog were having dinner with them. A cute keepsake, and I still cherish the picture to this day. And yes, Snoopy is smiling in the photo.

There was also a "test your dog's agility" activity. It included tests like running your dog through a cloth tube, walking your dog up a ramp and back down, and hurdles. I brought Snoopy over. We were greeted by a gregarious woman wearing a tee-shirt with her company's name on it. She ran the testing. She looked at Snoopy and loudly stated, "Oh, what a pretty dog." I never tired of hearing those words. Neither did he. Not that he knew he was pretty, but he could tell when someone was pleasant toward him, or had a pleasant energy.

Whenever someone compliments the *physical appearance* of a person's pet, they usually respond with a big smile and an even bigger "thank you," as if they had something to do with it. Unless you gave birth to your pet, I don't think so. I was always conscious of this and when Snoopy would get a compliment on his good looks, I would just agree with the person and smile.

Snoopy had an unbelievable natural agility for a dog that was never really trained in agility. It most likely had something to do with him being part Sheltie. Here's a perfect example...I would walk Snoopy near a brick wall that was part of a Warner Brothers building on Olive Avenue around the corner from our apartment. It was about three feet high, by two feet wide, and the length of one city block. I would give the command, "Snoopy, up!" and he would jump onto the wall. I'd walk alongside of it and he'd follow my pace. If I ran, he'd follow that pace. Sometimes he'd prance on the wall like a pony, or a little fox. After doing this a few times I didn't need to give a command anymore. He would automatically jump onto the wall, whenever he was near it. If anyone driving by saw this, their heads would turn and they'd slow in their cars to watch him.

I asked the woman doing the agility testing if Snoopy could take the ramp test. She asked if he had ever been on a ramp like hers, or had taken any agility training. I said, "No, not like yours and no formal training." She said, "Okay, but please be careful." The testing ramp was about four feet high, by 30 feet long, and only twelve inches wide.

I gave the command, "Snoopy, up!" and he started to move across the ramp. He moved slower than he did on the brick wall because he wasn't used to the height and narrowness of this ramp. The woman got nervous watching him, and ran alongside of him with her arms outreached to catch him in case he fell. I firmly said, "Don't do that, you'll make him fall." She backed away and Snoopy completed the length of the ramp. Then I got him to do it again in the opposite direction. I praised him and gave him a biscuit.

With a little coaxing, he ran through a fabric tube known as *the chute* that they use at dog shows. The woman was impressed with his agility ability, especially since he had no real training. I then took Snoopy over to the hurdles and tried to get him to jump over them. He had no interest in them whatsoever. He looked at me like, "No way can I do that. What do you think I am, a Border Collie?" I thanked the woman for letting Snoopy play and we moved on to another activity.

Next up...the doggy paw print booth. This was a fantastic way to get your dog's paw print without having to search for wet cement and a chisel. Each dog would have his or her paw placed in a small round block of clay-like substance. Following the gentleman's instructions, who ran the booth, I first placed Snoopy's right front paw print into a green non-toxic ink pad, then into the clay-like substance...and voila! I had his paw print. The roughly three-inch round block was then placed in a cardboard box with a lid, to protect it. I wrote Snoopy's name and the date on the box with a pen they provided. I still have this wonderful little keepsake of my best friend.

Snoopy's right front paw print

We walked around for a few more minutes. I grabbed a hamburger patty from the hamburger and hot dog stand provided to the human guests, and gave it to Snoopy as a special treat. He scarfed it down in seconds. It was time for the movie. The sight of at least 100 couches being used as seating for dogs and their owners, facing a giant outdoor movie screen, showing a dog cartoon about dogs, was truly wonderful.

I rushed to get us a couch. It was bit of a task making sure Snoopy *stayed* on the couch. He knew he wasn't allowed on the furniture at home, and here I was telling him it was okay to lie on a couch. Every time I put him on it, he'd jump off. I literally had to hold him down. After a few minutes he got the message it was okay and he relaxed. We watched the first 30 minutes of the movie, then left. I had seen it several times and didn't feel like sitting through it again. Snoopy didn't seem to mind. He neither protested, nor asked later, "What happened to *Lady and the Tramp*?" All in all, it was a fun time and a memory I will always hold dear to my heart.

-22-

HERB TOFU

For most of his life, Snoopy was one of the most calm, obedient dogs you'd ever meet. Other people seemed to agree. Friends would let me bring him to their parties where no other dogs were allowed. My hair stylist, who had a strict policy of no animals in the salon, would let Snoopy lie a few feet behind me and watch me get my hair cut.

There was something about him. It had nothing to do with me, it was in his nature. It went beyond being sweet and well-behaved. Many dogs are sweet and well-behaved. Snoopy had something in his energy people liked so much; they loved having him around. His energy was very good for me. On many occasions, he helped calm down my neurotic foolishness.

I could leave a plate of food on the coffee table in my living room, which was about level to his chest, and when I'd get up to go to the bathroom, it would all be there when I got back...except for the herb tofu.

Trader Joe's, a specialty retail grocery store where I had shopped, and still do, was selling an herb tofu product. It was a block of firm tofu with various herbs mixed in it—simply delicious—I loved it. One afternoon for lunch,

I made an open-faced herb tofu sandwich on whole-grain kamut bread. Snoopy's nostrils dilated upon smelling it, as I set it down on the coffee table to eat and watch TV. I firmly called out the command, "Go on, this is not for you! Go lie down!" and he did, like numerous times before.

I needed to go to the bathroom, so I went, having full confidence Snoopy would be lying in his favorite spot by the picture window when I got back. Boy, was I wrong. I hadn't been gone two minutes when I arrived back to eat my lunch. There was Snoopy, smacking his lips and scarfing down his last mouthful of my herb tofu sandwich on whole-grain kamut bread, on the living room carpet.

I was seriously upset. Not only was I hungry, and hungry for this specific sandwich, I was disappointed in him. I cleaned up the small amount on the carpet he hadn't eaten and yelled, "Bad dog" repeatedly for thirty seconds or so. He knew he had done wrong. It showed on his face, like an adolescent boy, who steals his dad's Playboy magazines and gets caught, but realizes it was worth it. I never left an open-faced herb tofu sandwich on whole-grain kamut bread within his reach again.

-23-

PIG BONE HOLIDAY TREAT AND VETERINARIANS

My next-door neighbor, Martha, a hardworking Cuban lady from Miami, lived across the hall from us. Well, it wasn't actually a hall; it was more like a concrete slab about a yard-square between our front doors. Martha was a single mom who shared her apartment with her teenage daughter and young son. She liked my boy Snoopy, and from time to time would take care of him when I went away if Virginia wasn't available. Martha's name was spelled like "Martha" and most people would assume it was pronounced *Mar-tha*. But she pronounced it *Marrr-ta*. You sort of rolled the "R" in her name and dropped the "H," more of a Spanish pronunciation.

One year on Christmas Day, she made a traditional Cuban dinner of roast pig, black beans and white rice, platanos, greens, and other goodies. Several of her friends and relatives came over to enjoy the festivities. After it was over, she stopped by and asked if Snoopy could have this huge bone from the roasted pig. I looked it over.

It looked like a small knucklebone on each end with a piece of one-inch thick bone about a foot long, connecting them. I had no idea what part of the pig it was from, but it looked strong. It looked like Snoopy would have a hard time tearing into it, and maybe it would clean his teeth. It was cooked, so he probably wouldn't go as berserk over it, like he had the raw knucklebone. I said okay. It would be a nice holiday treat. Not that he knew it was a holiday, but it's how I justified letting him eat something out of the norm. I laid a towel down on the carpet where I wanted him to eat it.

Snoopy went a little crazy for this bone, but not as crazy as the raw knucklebone. I would be able to take it from him whenever I wanted without a hassle. He tore into it for 30 minutes and chewed off any traces of meat. I then noticed he broke it in half in the center and was licking out whatever was inside. I said, "Okay, that's enough," and I took it from him without incident. He was smiling ear to ear. He sucked down the remainder in his mouth as he headed for his water bowl and drank what was left in it.

I examined the part of the bone he was licking. Inside it looked like uncooked fat. Was a pig so fatty that it contained fat in the center of its bones? I wasn't sure, but whatever Snoopy was licking out of that bone looked like some horrible stuff.

An hour later he was throwing up *and* had diarrhea. My poor baby...and my poor carpet. I called our vet, Dr. Carol Skaar, on her emergency number and left a message. Dr. Altman, our previous vet, had retired.

Dr. Skaar was also a class act like Dr. Altman; a caring lady with many years of experience. She was nice enough to get back to me right away, it being Christmas Day. She let me know cooked bones of any animal aren't safe because they splinter too easily and could get caught in his throat, or cause other problems. I hadn't known that, or I would have never let Snoopy have it. Dr. Altman had recommended raw knucklebones, but we never had a conversation about *cooked* animal bones, or I would have remembered.

Dr. Skaar suggested that for Snoopy's diarrhea I give him cooked hamburger meat with rice or potatoes, and for his upset stomach children's doses of Kaopectate®, also known as bismuth subsalicylate or "the pink stuff." Snoopy could barely get any of the food down, except for a tiny bit of the hamburger meat. Dr. Skaar was out of town until the next day. She said to call her then to give her an update on Snoopy's condition.

As the hours passed, Snoopy didn't seem to be getting better, and I was getting paranoid. I had to try something else. I called several emergency vet services. A holistic vet clinic in North Hollywood was open. The guy who answered the phone said he was a vet tech. I assumed his job was to give some kind of helpful advice, not to try and scare me.

I told him what happened with Snoopy. He went on and on about how dogs *die* from eating bones and things they shouldn't at holiday time, and to get over to his clinic right now before it was too late. I said, "Are you sure?" He said, "Oh, yeah, we had a couple dogs *die* just today from the very thing you're describing." I hung up on the jerk. He may have scared me a little, but I wasn't falling for his game. Snoopy was nowhere near death's door. He was still walking around okay. Eventually his involuntary puking and crapping became less frequent. My biggest concern was that he was barely eating, and he always ate like a pig dog. How ironic, he gets sick from eating pig. Snoopy didn't do well with pig. He had eaten a pig's ear that turned his poop to mush when he was a puppy, and now this. I learned my lesson. I never gave him any part of a pig again. Geez, I was born Jewish. I should have applied the part about not eating pork to Snoopy. After all, he was my son.

The next day, I brought him to Dr. Skaar. Her animal clinic in Burbank is called the Toluca Burbank Dog and Cat Hospital. Dr. Skaar was always, and still is, a great vet. While living in Burbank I took Snoopy to her for several years. She gave Snoopy an anti-diarrhea shot, a shot of antibiotics, and a ten day supply of oral antibiotics. Turns out he ate the one part of the pig bone, cooked or uncooked, that animals are not supposed to consume. Within 24 hours he was feeling so much better from the medication, and his diarrhea stopped completely. I don't know what was in the shot, but it worked like magic.

My neighbor, Martha, felt bad about the whole thing. I didn't blame her for it. It wasn't her fault. From her point of view she was being a good neighbor, and she was. It was that darn pig! He reached out from the dead and put a hurtin' on my boy. He should have saved it for the humans he gives heart attacks and high cholesterol. Dogs don't deserve any kind of pain or suffering.

I didn't forget about the vet tech jerk, who answered the phone at holistic vet clinic in North Hollywood. I called back a few days later, and got hold of the vet whose name was on the door, and told her what happened. I let her know she shouldn't have some nitwit working for her, spreading fear to potential new clients, especially during holiday time. She agreed, and apologized for the bad help. Who knows if it was a tactic she used to drum up business under the guise of being holistic? She wasn't going to tell me. At least I didn't fall for it.

A fun photo of our first Christmas together

In all the years Snoopy and I were together it was a rare occasion we went to a veterinarian. Other than when he was neutered and vaccinated as a pup, we went less than two dozen times in 13 years. I am not counting the several times he went to Dr. Skaar to get his nails trimmed, which wasn't an office visit.

I personally didn't trust most of them. I view most vets like AMA doctors. They treat the symptoms, not the cause. Many are well-meaning and highly-educated with years of schooling, but in today's world the all-mighty dollar can rule over their decisions with unnecessary expensive tests, shots, even surgeries. They have mortgages, kids to put through college, and whatnot. People sometimes forget that vets are running a business and they won't stay open very long by seeing your pet every two or three years. Many people blindly trust their vets without doing their own research. They let their emotions get in the way, which is understandable. I never wanted to see my boy ill or hurt in any way. I can understand more frequent visits if a pet has a genetic disorder, or disease, or has been in an accident.

I only took Snoopy when it was absolutely necessary; like when he ate something that got him sick, or he sprained his paw, or at the end of his life when it was crucial. I always fed him good quality dry dog food, no dairy products. I also supplemented his diet with lots of exercise, purified water and supplements like MSM, also known as "methylsulfonylmethane," a derivative of DMSO, which is a sulfur-based product used in veterinary medicine to relieve pain, along with glucosamine and chondroitin.

The first couple of years I was learning about Snoopy and common dog aliments, I had no clue what a "hot spot" was. Our first vet, Dr. Altman, had retired and I was in search of a new vet because Snoopy had an itch so bad on his front right leg that he was chewing the fur off. I hadn't found Dr. Skaar yet, and a friend recommended an animal hospital in Studio City, California which was only a few miles from me. I called and got Snoopy an appointment.

When we arrived I filled out the necessary paperwork. A few minutes later my name was called and an assistant led me and Snoopy into an exam room. We waited several more minutes and the vet entered. He was maybe thirty and had an air about him that was more clinical than caring. For some reason, when he tried to examine Snoopy's leg, Snoopy backed away from him and cowered in a corner of the room. He wouldn't let this vet touch him. He didn't growl at the guy, he just didn't like him. I had to comfort Snoopy and hold out his leg for him to examine it. The vet knew what most people who had experience with dogs knew. It was a hot spot; possibly caused by a number of things—from a flea bite, to an allergic reaction, to boredom.

Realizing Snoopy didn't like him, the vet had a vet tech clean Snoopy's leg and wrap it. He then suggested I keep it wrapped for several days and put some Bitter Apple on the bandage so he wouldn't tear it off. Bitter Apple is topical spray that discourages dogs from biting and chewing on hot spots. Then the vet started telling me how Snoopy was a *very* nervous dog and he would like to prescribe Prozac. *Doggie Prozac?* I looked at him like he's nuts. He saw my dog for five minutes for a hot spot and wanted to put him on a psychotropic drug. What was he smoking? I flat out refused and politely left with Snoopy. No wonder Snoopy wouldn't let this so-called veterinarian touch him, he didn't trust him...and after our conversation, neither did I. A good veterinarian, like a good Western medical doctor, is hard to find.

-24-

MELVIN AND
THE DIM-WITTED
COCKER SPANIEL

Wendy and I had been dating a couple years when she and Melvin moved in with me and Snoopy. Melvin and Snoopy were best friends, buddies, pals. I had heard of dogs and cats living together and getting along, but it was the first time I had ever experienced it.

Melvin was a 100-percent indoor cat. So much so that if you carried him outside of our apartment, away from his comfy environment to the unknown outdoors, he'd practically claw through your arms and back to get back inside. His fear of the outdoors was fine with me. I didn't want to have to worry about him getting into a fight with street cats, or a dog getting loose and going after him, or any number of scenarios.

I had befriended several neighbors on our block that had dogs. One neighbor, Lauren, a pixie-sized actress in her early-twenties, was the owner of an adorable male Cocker Spaniel. He and Snoopy would play from time to time, when they'd run into each other on the street. This Cocker

Spaniel was a very sweet dog, like most Cockers, but in all honesty, he was a few Bradys short of a Bunch.

One day I saw him with a cast on his front leg. I asked Lauren what had happened. She said they were driving in her car, she rolled down the window for him to get some air, which most dogs love, and he jumped out the window. I asked how fast she was going. She said, "25 miles per hour."

I said, "You're joking, right?"

"No, he jumped out of the window at 25 miles per hour and broke his leg."

I had never heard of such a thing, and I was a bit shocked by it. I expressed my true concern and made comments like, "Glad he's okay," "He's lucky he didn't get run over," "Poor dog." But part of me was thinking, "This is the most dim-witted dog in the world. What a klutz. Didn't he sense the car was moving? How dense could he be? You should contact the *Guinness Book of World Records* and see if he qualifies for World's Klutziest Dog." I love dogs. But this dog was as smart as a stick.

Melvin seemed to have no fear of dogs. Of course he knew Snoopy would never hurt him. Snoopy was too gentle to go after another animal for no reason. But one day...he had a reason.

One afternoon, I ran into Lauren and asked if Dim-Witted Cocker Spaniel liked cats. Of course I didn't call him dim-witted to her face. She says, "Oh, yeah, he loves cats, I have a cat too. They get along great." Then I asked if Dim-Witted Cocker Spaniel would like to meet our cat Melvin. She said yes. I brought them upstairs to the apartment. Dim-Witted Cocker Spaniel and Melvin seemed to get along at first. He sniffed Melvin and Melvin let him, which was a good sign. Snoopy carefully watched this go down. He seemed okay with it. Suddenly, Dim-Witted Cocker Spaniel became aggressive and gave Melvin, a spastic-like head-butt.

It scared Melvin. He ran into the bedroom and jumped up on the bed, where he felt safe. Snoopy never jumped on the bed when they would play. It's where Melvin would go when he wanted to get away from him. Snoopy would bark at him to come down and continue playing, and Melvin would look at him like, "Yeah, right. Like that's gonna happen."

So, Melvin must have assumed all dogs must not jump on the bed. Sorry, Melvin. Dim-Witted Cocker Spaniel jumped up on the bed, and made another aggressive move toward him.

Wendy and I were freaking out. Snoopy was barking. Melvin hopped off the bed, ran past us and into the hallway, with Dim-Witted Cocker Spaniel in pursuit. Lauren yells "don't do that!" as if he was going to listen. Snoopy stopped Dim-Witted Cocker Spaniel cold in his tracks by grabbing the fur on his back with his teeth, and biting down.

He growled and shook Dim-Witted Cocker Spaniel like a rag doll. Now, Lauren was freaking out. I was in shock, watching my sweet boy acting like a wild beast, putting a beat-down on this dog for messing with his cat buddy.

I carefully grabbed Snoopy by his collar and yelled, "Snoopy, stop!" He let Dim-Witted Cocker Spaniel go, smiled, and gave him a look of, "Don't come into my house and mess with my buddy Melvin ever again. Are we still friends?" Dim-Witted Cocker Spaniel remained still and was panting heavily. Lauren looked him over. There was no blood or wounds on his body, just a bunch of Snoopy's slobber. It was merely a warning. Needless to say, Lauren and her Dim-Witted Cocker Spaniel never came over to our place again.

-25-

MORE NEIGHBORHOOD DOGS

In addition to Lauren and the Dim-witted Cocker Spaniel, there were other dogs and neighbors that Snoopy and I would come in contact with. Loni, an attractive, semi-pushy Jewish American Princess in her late-thirties, lived two apartment buildings down from us with her two Pomeranian pooches. She loved these little dogs and was quite the protective Jewish Mama. She usually carried one under each arm. They looked like extensions of her armpits. Whenever Snoopy would see them while we were out and about, he'd want to play.

Loni liked Snoopy. She'd carefully place her Pomeranians on the ground, and the three of them would play on a patch of grass behind her apartment building. They would sniff each other and run around. Every now and then Loni would get overprotective, thinking Snoopy was *being too aggressive*, which he never was, but she felt him barking too close to her babies was a sign of aggressiveness. She'd reach down, scoop them back up under her armpits, and ask if I could please take Snoopy away. I would oblige, put him on-leash and leave. No sense in arguing about how dogs sometimes bark when they play.

There was another woman in her mid-twenties, who lived on the street behind us, very small in stature, with a male Great Dane. One of my nosy neighbors told me she inherited the dog when her boyfriend left her. This dog was huge. It would practically drag its new, little owner down the street when she took him for a walk. My nosy neighbor also told me this Great Dane bit a dog in the neighborhood, on the back, and its victim had to be taken to the vet for stitches.

How anyone could keep a dog that big in a small two-bedroom apartment was crazy to me. I did not want this big dog anywhere near Snoopy. Its bark was so loud and guttural; it sounded like it came from a monster in Sci-Fi movie. He made me nervous.

Once, I was walking Snoopy past their apartment, the Great Dane was inside and he sensed Snoopy outside. Through an open window, he let out several of his loud, guttural barks. Snoopy took off running, pulling me on his leash. Poor baby was scared. I didn't know what the Great Dane communicated to Snoopy, but it definitely was not an invite to a Dodger game. Thankfully, the woman and the Great Dane moved away shortly after that. I did not want to have to deal with them.

Then there was Ray, the mentally unbalanced guy, and his elderly male German Shepherd. I have nothing against all the good mentally challenged folks in the world. However, Ray was neither good, nor remotely friendly. Not only was he mentally off, he was drunk most of the time. Ray was skinny, in his thirties, but looked more like he was in his fifties. He shaved his head and always had about a week's growth that matched his beard stubble. He would talk to himself in a raspy, alcoholic smoker's voice, reminiscent of a blues singer, as he walked his dog several times a day around the block. He rented a small apartment at the end of our block from an elderly woman who owned the building and took pity on him. Everything about Ray was not the norm. He named his dog Ray Junior.

I, as well as many others feel their dog is like a son or daughter, a real member of their immediate family, but no way was I naming my dog Joey Junior. To this day I've never heard of anyone naming a dog after themselves, other than Ray.

The German Shepherd, or Ray Jr., rather, was a good twelve years old, which was fairly old for a 80 pound dog of his breed. He was arthritic and would follow several feet behind Ray Sr. without a leash on his daily and nightly walks. The one feature that stood out about the poor old fella; his tail stuck out straight all the time. It didn't bend or wag. It looked like an eighteen inch fur stick coming out of his rear end. I later found out from Ray Sr.'s landlord, Ray Jr.'s tail had been broken. It never healed correctly and that was the result.

How does a dog break its tail? What did Ray Sr. did to this poor animal? I didn't want to know. I kept Snoopy away from Ray Sr. and Jr. On the rare occasion we were walking in the neighborhood at the same time, Snoopy would bark at Ray Sr.; Ray Jr. wouldn't even acknowledge Snoopy. I'm not sure, but he might have been deaf.

One day, I found out that Ray Jr. had died. I realized this when I saw Ray Sr. walking a *new* male German Shepherd, about a year old. He named his new dog, you guessed it...Ray Jr. Maybe he should have called him Ray

Jr. the second, or the third, or the fourth, or the fifth. Who knows how many dogs he named after himself?

As I observed Ray Sr. walking this new dog, it was the strangest thing. New Ray Jr., had a look on his face like he wanted to get away from his new owner. The dog knew his new master wasn't all there. My neighbor, Claudia, told me poor old Ray Jr. had to be put down; he was sick and in too much pain from arthritis. She helped Ray Sr. get his new dog.

Right away too. Ray Sr. didn't even mourn the loss of his old best friend for 24 hours, and he had a new dog. Claudia was very helpful. She gave Ray Sr. his new Ray Jr.; paid for his adoption, license and neutering fees. What a sweetheart. She felt sorry for him. This new German Shepherd had just come into the shelter, and she felt he was a good fit for him. If she didn't do this for Ray Sr., I doubt anyone, or any organization would have let him have a dog. He was barely able to take care of himself, being drunk most of the time.

One afternoon I saw Ray Sr. walking new Ray Jr. across the street from my apartment where two boys were playing. These boys were little delinquents, and they were only about eight or nine years old. One of them once told me to go "you know what" myself, as I was walking to my car. I was taken aback. I didn't know this kid. I yelled, "Come here! I want to talk to you!" I moved toward him and he ran off. I knocked on the door of the apartment he shared with his mother, and told her what he said. She was a Hispanic woman in her late-twenties wearing cheap makeup. She calmly replied in a thick accent, "Oh, he's got ADD." Like it was no big deal, like he swore at strange men all the time. I said, "He needs to watch his mouth around adults. He's going to say what he said to me, to some guy, who's going to beat up the crap out of him, or worse." She didn't respond to my comments, so I left. A-D-D: *Attention Deficit Disorder*. I should've said it's not ADD that caused your son to swear at an adult he doesn't know. It's B-P: Bad Parenting.

So this punk and his friend were playing on the front lawn of the apartment building where they lived. Ray Sr. and new Ray Jr. were walking by. These two punks started calling Ray Sr. "spazz" and "tardo" and made fun of the way he looked and talked. Ray Sr. started yelling and swearing at them. New Ray Jr. barked at them. Then Ray Sr. yelled, "Sic 'em" and let go of new Ray Jr.'s leash. New Ray Jr. ran straight for those punks. They took off running between the nearby apartment buildings, probably to get a baseball bat, or a gun. Ray Sr. thought this was the funniest thing he'd ever seen. He keeled over on the sidewalk, laughing nonstop like a seal on caffeine.

New Ray Jr. followed the punks for a few feet, and then wandered around on their front lawn. He suddenly got a look on his face of, "Hey, my crazy master's not holding on to me," and he started to walk along the sidewalk away from Ray Sr. Ray Sr. recovered from laughing, when he realized new Ray Jr. was several buildings away. He yelled, "C'mere!" and attempted to get hold of his leash, but new Ray Jr. was no dummy. He took off running down the block; he wanted to be free from his demented owner. Ray Sr. yelled again, "C'mere!" and chased after him. New Ray Jr. wasn't listening. I watched him run around the corner with Ray Sr. in pursuit. Now, I was laughing.

A couple weeks later, I was walking Snoopy past the apartment building where Ray Sr. and new Ray Jr. lived. It was an older building with side-by-side apartments, built in the 1920s. Ray Sr.'s apartment door had been left wide open and no one was around. I moved toward it and looked inside. It was disgusting. Ray Sr. slept on a dirty old mattress on the floor. There was very little furniture, no bathroom or kitchen that I could see, and clothes and garbage were scattered everywhere.

His place was much smaller than a single-sized apartment. Maybe a ten foot by ten foot room; unfit for one person, let alone a man and a big dog. No wonder new Ray Jr. had that look on his face and had been trying to get away from his new master.

I called the Burbank Animal Shelter to report what I saw. They didn't mess around. They showed up the following day to check out new Ray Jr.'s living space. I don't know if Ray Sr. or his landlady were fined, but the following week I saw the place being cleaned and painted. I did my good deed for the poor dog. He couldn't help who adopted him.

Eventually there was a good turnout for new Ray Jr. and his owner. Ray Sr. was forced into a long-term rehabilitation facility by his family, to get help with his alcoholism, and they didn't take dogs. New Ray Jr. was sent back to the Burbank Animal Shelter. Claudia told me she got him adopted by a family with a house and a big backyard. Good for him. Ray Sr. probably missed his dog very much, but considering the circumstances, what happened was really the best thing for both of them. New Ray Jr. got a new loving home, and Ray Sr. got a new start on a better life.

There were other characters in my old Burbank 'hood. Like the old Curmudgeonly Guy, who most mornings watched people walk their dogs past his apartment building to make sure none of them crapped on the lawn. Whenever

I'd see him, I'd walk Snoopy very quickly past his building to avoid any confrontation. Curmudgeonly Guy was in his late-sixties, most likely lived on Social Security benefits and had nothing better to do with his time. It wasn't even his lawn, he was a renter. He was a bit of a nut.

One morning, I didn't see Curmudgeonly Guy watching and Snoopy took a dump on his lawn. I picked it up with one of the several plastic bags I always kept in my back pants pockets. As we were walking away, I saw Curmudgeonly Guy run from the side of the building, walk over to where Snoopy dumped and examine the area.

He pointed to the ground, and screamed at me, "Hey, what about the residual!?" Residual poop from my dog's dump? What was this dimwit talking about? I was able to pick up all of it. Snoopy's dumps were extremely firm. I never fed him wet food, only high quality dry...and pig parts were a thing of the past.

Before I answered, I quickly summed up Curmudgeonly Guy. He was a good 25 years older than me, about five-feet, nine inches tall with a medium build. He had the energy of the school bully, who thinks he's smart, but is really not too bright. I figured I could take this guy, even if he had some kind of fighting flashback from his youth and wanted to get it on. I put on my best psycho face, and yelled, "Why don't you lick it up!?" Then I looked him in the eye. He didn't answer. He quickly turned away and went into his apartment, where he should have been in the first place. After that, he never said a word to me. Even though I was crudely joking with Curmudgeonly Guy, I got my desired result; to walk Snoopy around the block in peace.

-26-

THE OLD BLACK LAB

There was an elderly gentleman in the neighborhood I'd run in to from time to time. I'm guessing he must have been in his mid-seventies. He always dressed casually in short-sleeved shirts, black jeans, and penny loafers. He lived-in and owned two four-unit buildings on Maple Street, directly behind the apartment I lived in.

He had an old male black Lab that he'd walk every day. The poor dog was getting on in years and moved very slowly. Around the dog's face, his fur had aged, making him look like he was sporting a gray beard. He was a sweet, mellow boy.

Snoopy liked him. He would sniff him, then crouch down on his front legs, look up at him and bark, in an attempt to get him to play. Old black Lab would get excited the best he could, wag his tail and shake a bit, from the thrill of having my young pup's energy cross his path. The elderly gentleman liked that his dog became more alive when Snoopy came around. He hadn't seen his dog that active in a long time. We'd usually chat for a few moments about our dogs, the weather, or the goings-on in the neighborhood, and we'd be on our way. This went on for about a year or so.

At that time, I never thought about Snoopy being old one day, like his dog. I was enjoying him for the young pup he was, and the fact I had my own dog again after thirty years. A few months passed and I ran into the elderly gentleman again. He was without his old black Lab.

I asked where the Lab was. He said he had to put him down several weeks ago. I told him I was sorry for his loss. He looked *soooo* sad. Later in our conversation, he said something that has never left me, but when he said it, I didn't understand the real depth and meaning of it until many years later.

In our conversation, I nonchalantly asked if he were going to get another dog. He paused for a moment, then looked at me and said, "No...I can't take the pain." It was too painful for him to see a dog he loved so much, and had all its life, die. To go through something like that again would hurt too much. I couldn't relate to those six words at the time. I didn't have the experience of losing a dog I had cared for its whole life, like he did. It wasn't until I lost Snoopy, after more than thirteen years of being together, did his words take on a new meaning. I too may not get another dog. No...I can't take the pain.

-27-

A MOTORIZED TOY TRUCK, A MACAW, A MINIATURE HORSE, AND SHEEP

Snoopy loved, loved, loved to chase motorized toys. Yes, motorized toys. I discovered this because my downstairs neighbor, Jordan, had a wireless motorized toy truck with remote control. It looked like a monster truck shrunk down to the size of a long shoebox. It was about eighteen inches long by eight inches wide, and this thing was fast. I didn't read the specs on it, but it seemed like it ran up to twenty miles per hour. Jordan was a strapping lad in his mid-twenties, from the Pacific Northwest, who liked to hack cable TV and give it to everyone in our building for free. He also liked Snoopy and always gave him a hearty, "Hey, Snoopy!" every time he saw him and took time to pet him.

One summer afternoon I put Snoopy on-leash and we went downstairs to go for a walk. Jordan was in front of our building with his motorized toy truck, running it up and down the street, along the sidewalk and nearby driveways. Snoopy saw it and went *wild*. He pulled on his leash, barking and whining, dying to get at it.

For some reason this toy truck got him more energized than seeing silver squirrels in Chicago. I didn't know what it was. The sound of the motor? The size of it? The movement? Whatever it was, it drove an instinct in him to go after it. I asked Jordan if I could let Snoopy off-leash to chase it. No problem. It could be fun. I removed the leash from his collar. He went after this thing like it was a raw knucklebone with dried pig ears on beef-flavored wheels. He barked at it, snapped at the wheels and body with his teeth, trying to get hold of it. Wherever it went, Snoopy went.

Jordan would spin the truck in circles, around corners, and up and down the sidewalk. Snoopy never took his eyes off it. He was mesmerized by it...and for some reason *the way* he chased it, looked funny. Snoopy's head kept moving up and down like a bobble head dog toy. It made us laugh. I was laughing so hard, I was losing my breath. Jordan tried to control his laughter while maneuvering it. He would then stop the truck and Snoopy would stand next to it, barking at it; like he was demanding it give him an answer. To what, I don't know. Then Jordan would move it along again and Snoopy would be right on its tail, and we'd laugh.

Snoopy must have run after this toy truck a good twenty minutes before Jordan stopped it and put it away. Snoopy was worn out, panting heavily, his tongue hanging out, badly needing water. No need for a walk after all that. I took him upstairs and he quickly gulped down a bowl and a half of water. The novelty of him chasing this truck didn't wear off. We did this with Jordan several times. A good run for Snoopy and a good gut-busting laugh for us.

Our neighborhood had various characters coming and going through it. While out one afternoon playing with Snoopy in back of my apartment building, a "new-agey" woman in an embroidered denim jacket was cutting through the gate to the street behind us. It was a shortcut meant for the residents of the surrounding buildings, but from time to time non-residents would use it. The woman had a beautiful red, yellow, and blue Macaw on her shoulder.

Snoopy immediately started whining; wanting to play with it, or at least get closer to it—get a better whiff. At this point, a couple of my neighbors, who were doing laundry in the nearby laundry room, came out to see the bird. They asked questions and petted him, and he would make loud noises every now and then. In between the woman answering questions and the neighbors wooing and awing over the bird, I asked if Snoopy could get a little closer to her Macaw, to smell it. I said he liked birds. She said okay and leaned down her shoulder with the bird on it about a foot, while being preoccupied with the neighbors.

To my surprise, Snoopy reached his head up and snapped at the Macaw's tail feathers, getting a few small ones in his mouth in the process. Holy crapola! I quickly pulled him back by his collar. No one seemed to notice what he did and the Macaw didn't even flinch. I quickly moved Snoopy along and got him out of there. He didn't want to play with the Macaw; *he thought it was food.* After that, I did my best to keep him away from birds.

Another time, on a Sunday morning after breakfast, Wendy and I took Snoopy for a walk in a neighborhood adjacent to the Los Angeles Equestrian Center in Burbank, which was walking distance from our apartment. I have no idea why it's located in Burbank. I doubt if you'll find a Burbank Equestrian Center located anywhere in Los Angeles.

This neighborhood was zoned for horses. Many of the homes had stables in their backyards. As we walked along the sidewalk on a quiet residential street, admiring the beautiful homes and landscape, up ahead about twenty yards was a sight I'll never forget. A young couple was walking their male Miniature Horse toward us, on a leash attached to its harness.

I'd never seen a Miniature Horse up close, only on TV, and neither had Wendy. As we got closer to them, I could see that he was maybe three feet tall. He was stunning. His coat was a shiny chestnut brown and he was perfectly proportioned. Snoopy had no clue what this animal was. He had interacted with various dogs and cats, birds, squirrels, horses, possums, even a raccoon he spotted in a tree one day. He had also observed fish swimming in an aquarium in a pet store. But what was this new odd creature coming toward him?

The owners were very nice and answered our questions about their beautiful boy and let us pet him. He was serene and calm. Of course Snoopy wanted to play with him. He turned his neck in a curious manner and looked at him like, "What the heck are you?" Then he sniffed him all around, got in a crouching position and started barking at the little fella. It was a playful bark and the Miniature Horse didn't seem to mine. Most likely he'd been around dogs. He just sort of stood there with his owners. I pulled Snoopy back and told him to knock it off...and he did. There wasn't much else to say or do. I would have loved to have seen the two of them play together in a grassy backyard or a corral, but these were not people we knew. I thanked them for their time, letting us say "hi" to their beautiful boy, and we continued on our walk. It was a memorable morning.

I did get to test Snoopy's herding instinct with sheep. On a chilly Saturday winter morning, well...chilly for Burbank, I drove to a ranch in Antelope Valley in north Los Angeles County, run by a dog herding club. It was a 45 minute drive from Burbank. In the winter the temperature in Antelope Valley would get down below 40 degrees, which is cold for Southern California. I paid a $30.00 assessment fee. The only qualification other than the fee; your dog had to be all or part of a herding breed, which ranged from Border collies, to German Shepherds, to Shetland sheepdogs. If your dog had the word "Sheepdog" or "Collie" in its breed's name, he or she could get an instinct test. I had a feeling that the people who ran the place may have been letting people slide on the breed qualification thing. I could have sworn I saw a Shar Pei, who from the neck down looked like he was wearing a fake fur coat made to look like an Old English sheepdog. I stayed away from it.

The process was simple. You waited in line with a bunch of dogs and their owners, and one dog at a time they'd have the dog's owner bring his or her dog into an enclosed arena, which was about a quarter-acre lot. Then a trainer brought out a small flock of sheep, maybe three or four, from behind a wooden fence where they were kept, to gauge your dog's level of "willingness to work," meaning: does your dog have it in them to chase sheep? I watched a few German Shepherds and a couple of other herding breeds I didn't recognize, one after the other, chase after the sheep as they were being lead around by the trainer with a herding stick.

I felt sorry for the sheep. The same small flock was used all day long. They looked worn out, ready for a nap.

It was finally Snoopy's turn. I brought him into the enclosed arena. The tired-looking sheep were brought out and the trainer got them to run around like...well...sheep. Snoopy couldn't have cared less. He looked at them like they smelled bad, which they did. Then he wandered around and sniffed the ground.

The trainer, a man about forty, who had the energy of a used car salesman desperate for a sale, gave Snoopy a command to go after the sheep. Snoopy barely acknowledged his existence and went back to sniffing the ground. I got frustrated. I had not driven all the way out to this ranch in Antelope Valley, in the freezing cold, to have him sniff dirt. What happened to his built-in Sheltie herding instinct?

I ran over to him, pointed and yelled, "Go on! Get 'em! Get 'em! Get those sheep!" At first, Snoopy moved slowly toward them. Then he started running at their heels and they moved around the arena for a few seconds. He stopped and the sheep stopped. I yelled again and he chased them again. This routine continued for a couple more minutes and his time was up. I put him back on-leash and led him out of the arena. We got back in line and did it two more times. The assessment fee included three rounds of herding attempts.

I didn't like any of this and Snoopy seemed bored through the whole process. The people that ran the place told me how *great* he was and wanted me to sign him up for herding classes. No, thank you! They were a legitimate organization and they may have meant well, but the whole thing felt kind of shady to me. The sheep were trained to run. I could have placed a gerbil in the arena and if it got close enough to those sheep, they would have run from it. The worst part was that Snoopy smelled like sheep and was covered in dust and dirt. I put him in the car and took him home. It was time for a bath.

-28-

BATH TIME

Baths were never really a problem with Snoopy for most of his life. He was so obedient. With a little coaxing, he'd come into the bathroom with me, and I'd close the door behind us. He knew there was no getting out without his bath. I'd tap the tub with an open hand and give the command, "Snoopy, up!" and he would jump in the tub. Wherever we lived, in each bathroom stall I installed a hand-held shower head with an attached hose. It also came in handy when it was time to clean the bathtub and stall.

The way I washed Snoopy wasn't technically a bath. It was more of a shower, or what the animal grooming business calls a "dog wash." I never filled the tub with water. First, I would run the water and make sure it was just the right temperature, medium warm to the touch, never hot.

After I'd get Snoopy good and wet, I'd shake the shampoo bottle, flip open the cap, hold it over him and squeeze a line of it along his body. The thick liquid would hit his fur. I'd massage it in, getting him good and soapy all over, making sure not to get any in his eyes or mouth. Then I'd run the water again, get it back to right temperature and rinse him off.

When Snoopy's thick fur was wet and flush against his body it showed his musculature. He was average weight for a dog of his size and breeding, but having such a thick fluffy coat he appeared wider than he was. From time to time people would comment that he looked overweight, but they were merely seeing the thickness of his coat. To give them a better idea of his actual size, I would push down his fur with both my hands to show them how much smaller he was underneath. It's like when a person is wearing several layers of winter clothing; you can't really tell what their body looks like until they remove some of it.

I always washed Snoopy with a natural shampoo that contained essential oils. It was called Buddy Wash. I loved this stuff. The ingredients were purer than most natural shampoos sold to humans, and Snoopy always smelled clean and fresh afterwards without that chemical smell that comes from most dog shampoos. Geez, I sound like a commercial. But honestly, it was incredible stuff. I used it on him even in the later years of his life. On occasion, when I had him groomed, I'd bring it along and insist the groomer use it.

After bathing, or showering, rather, it was a process to get him dry. His fur would retain a lot of water. Some of it was so thick and long, I'd have to squeeze it out with both hands as if I were wringing out a furry wash cloth. Then I would dry him off with a towel or two. Never a blow dryer. After his first experience at the groomer as a pup, where he crapped himself because the noise frightened him, I didn't want him to experience that kind of anxiety again. With his blood flowing from the warm water having pulsated on his body for twenty minutes or so; he would run through the house jazzed up, like a happy puppy on some sort of doggie stimulant. He'd ram his snout into the carpet, roll over on his back several times and shake the remaining water off his fur. I always rewarded him for being such a good boy with a biscuit or two, which he'd happily gobble up.

Snoopy always liked baths. He'd smile all the while I was giving them to him. I guess the feeling of dirt coming off his body along with the love of his master made him feel even more of a special boy than he already was. I always did my best to turn bath time into fun time.

Snoopy loved taking baths

-29-

OUR NEW HOME AND NEIGHBORS WITH PETS

I had lived in same two-bedroom apartment in Burbank for about ten years. Many life-changing events happened there. I had adopted Snoopy into my life. Wendy and I were living together in a committed relationship, and were married in August 2002. We also had Melvin the cat.

In February of 2005, we decided to move to a new place. We were tired of our apartment and change would do us all good. Snoopy was now about eight years old, Melvin about six.

After much searching, I found us a beautiful two bedroom apartment in a fairly new building. It was laid out with the bedrooms upstairs, which reminded me of a condo. It was located on Hortense Street near Lankershim Boulevard, two miles west of our Burbank apartment in an area called Toluca Lake Adjacent. Technically it was in North Hollywood, but since some people tend to look down on North Hollywood as a less than desirable place to live, for marketing purposes they called it Toluca Lake Adjacent. It was on the border of Toluca Lake, California, a very desirable, upscale area of the Valley. Toluca Lake is famous for its Lakeside Golf Course, and being home to numerous celebrities since 1923; from Amelia Earhart, to Bob Hope, to Denzel Washington.

Moving was stressful. Being in one place for ten years, I had accumulated a lot of stuff. Things I didn't need, I sold at a yard sale. Whatever didn't sell, I donated to a women's shelter. It would not only be a major adjustment for Wendy and me, but for Snoopy and Melvin as well. I had been told cats could wig out during moving and that they sometimes hid in various places and it might take a while for them to get acclimated to their new surroundings.

With Melvin, nothing was further from what I was told. Once we moved in, he was like a kitten discovering a cardboard box for the first time. He ran around the apartment like it was an obstacle course. Going up and down the stairs, jumping on top of our moving boxes, watching us unpack; he was all over the place. Snoopy, who I assumed would have no issues with the new place, was overwhelmed and uncertain of his new surroundings. He didn't know what was going on. I had to coax him up the front steps of the building entrance *and* up the stairs in our apartment. It took about two weeks before he got into the groove of his new home.

Living in a new residence and neighborhood meant meeting new neighbors and their pets. The guy in the apartment next-door, a skinny dude in his twenties with jet-black dyed hair, tattoos, and a falsetto voice, was the owner of a black-and-white male Boston terrier. His dog had a hectic energy and a high-pitched bark that could get on your nerves real quick. His moods were all over the place, as if he were jacked up on steroids. The dog's name was Joey.

It was the first time I met a dog with my name. Well, not *my* name, the same name. It's probably more of a common occurrence if your name happens to be Skippy or Spike, or Jake. I suppose Joey is as good as any. People have the right to name their dog or cat whatever they want. Our cat's name is *Melvin*. However, you may have gone too far in trying to find your dog or cat a memorable name if you choose Caligula, Hitler, Stalin, John Wayne Gacy, Satan, or Karl Rove.

This dog Joey *loved* Snoopy. Snoopy...did...not...like...him. He'd greet Snoopy with a *yip-yip-yip-yip*, then jump on his head and face with his front paws and never-been-trimmed nails. Snoopy would get instantly upset and growl and snip at Joey. Those nails must have hurt. I'd pull Snoopy away, but Joey never got the message to back-off. He kept coming at Snoopy like a deranged boxer. I mentioned to Joey's owner that he might want to get Joey's nails trimmed. He said, "I'll look into it." He never did. It got to the point whenever I saw Joey coming our way I'd walk Snoopy in the opposite direction.

Snoopy and I became well-acquainted with our new neighborhood. We'd meet various people, and people with their pets. Snoopy would sniff out cats as we walked. He'd tug on his leash and let out his more-than-familiar puppy whine—though he was far from being a puppy anymore—and lead me toward bushes, underneath parked cars, trees, fences, on top of garbage cans—anywhere cats would hide—and every time, without failure, a cat would be right where he wanted to go. He wanted to play with them, like he did with Melvin.

Most outdoor cats are not like Melvin. Not only did

they *not* want to play, they were usually fearful of dogs, especially those out on the streets. Whenever Snoopy would do his puppy whine and tug on the leash, I'd make sure not to let him get too close to the cat's location. The last thing I wanted was a cat lashing out with its claws, and tearing into his sweet face.

Once I let him get close to a street cat. One day on our morning walk, a pretty black-and-white cat was slowly walking up a residential driveway as we moved along the adjacent sidewalk. The cat saw Snoopy and heard him whining. It didn't run. It showed no fear. He or she was curious about Snoopy. It looked at him with a blasé cat attitude of, "What are you all about? And maybe, or maybe not, do I care that you exist." Snoopy stopped whining. I sensed the cat was okay with him. I let Snoopy get about four feet from the cat. If the cat decided to go psycho I had enough room to pull him out of harm's way and get between them. They continued to look at each other. Snoopy's nostrils dilated as he smelled every inch of this cat.

Standing off to my left, about twenty feet away, was the cat's owner. I didn't notice him at first. He lived in the house the cat stopped in front of. He stood there wide-eyed, watching his cat with my dog. Then I heard him say two words, "That's amazing." He told me that his cat, a she, usually ran any time a dog got anywhere near her. If she saw a dog in the distance, she was gone. I told him that Snoopy loved cats in a good way, and most likely his cat sensed that he'd never hurt her. We chatted for a few minutes, he petted Snoopy, I said, "Take care," and we continued our walk.

One dog in the neighborhood I really, really, really adored, other than mine of course, was a purebred male

Collie, who lived on the corner of our street. It was one of the most gorgeous Collies I've ever seen, better looking than any Lassie on TV. Only ten months old, he constantly ran around his gated front yard.

Whenever I'd walk by with Snoopy, he'd go crazy, wanting to play with him, and they'd sniff each other through the metal fence. I'd reach over and pet him any chance I could. He was such a pretty and friendly pup. Snoopy, being part Sheltie, looked like he might be part Collie, which some people would assume when they would try to guess his mix of breeds.

Our new apartment and neighborhood were a great change of pace. After living in one place for so long I enjoyed the feeling of being in a new area and discovering everything it had to offer. Snoopy liked it, too.

-30-

CAR ACCIDENT NUMBER ONE AND BETTY THE JUNKYARD CAT

I donated my car; a fully loaded 1988 Buick Electra, to one of those "Donate your car to charity" companies on TV. It was a big, old, fun cruiser, but it was on its last legs. I had already pumped way too much cash into it, and it felt like more problems were on the way. I took the tax write off they offered.

I shopped around for a new set of wheels and bought a cherry 1998 Toyota Camry LE with 66,000 miles on it. This was 2005. A seven year old car in traffic-ridden Los Angeles with only 66,000 miles on it was a real find. That averaged out to 9428 miles a year, which is considered *very low* mileage for Southern California. Plus, I got it at a great price.

I bought it from a private owner in the Valley who babied it. I loved this car, it was pretty much flawless. It was emerald green and it had mag wheels—not a scratch on it. After about a week of owning it I decided to take a ride out to visit my cousin. She lived about 60 miles south of me, in Lake Forest, California, an upscale bedroom community in Orange County. It would be my first opportunity to drive my new car on the freeway for an extended period of time. It was Sunday morning. Wendy, Snoopy, and I got in the car and headed on down.

The drive was smooth, not much traffic. As we continued on the 5 Freeway South past Disneyland, I drove into the far left-hand Diamond Lane, also known as a carpool lane, intended for two or more passengers. I was cruising at about 65 miles per hour. About 40 yards ahead, on the shoulder of the freeway and only *a few feet* from the Diamond lane, were three or four large cement blocks. They were about ten feet long, by three feet high, and one foot wide. Why were they still there? There was no construction going on. They made me nervous.

I didn't want to hit them. So I slowed a bit as I drove by them, being extra careful with my new car. As I increased my speed, I misjudged the curve ahead and lost control of the steering wheel for just a fraction of a second. I hit the center divider on an angle with the front driver's side of my car at a good 55 miles per hour. Both front airbags went off, hitting Wendy and me in the face and chest. My foot hit the brake pedal, and my car kept moving for several yards, as the driver's side scraped along the center divider, and it tore into the emerald paint and steel body, before coming to complete stop. The powder from the airbags practically had me gagging.

Poor Snoopy, who was lying in the backseat, went flying into the back of my padded bucket seat and landed on the carpeted floorboard behind me. He was fine. Wendy wasn't hurt at all. I was okay, except I was in a bit of a daze and not too happy about having my new car totaled. At least no one was injured. That was the most important thing.

Driving into a divider on the freeway was a strange sensation. As the accident was happening; it didn't feel like *an accident* to me. It had the feeling of being on an amusement park ride that came to an abrupt stop.

As I put Snoopy on-leash and got him out of the wreckage, a Good Samaritan driver stopped to see if we were okay. I told him we were all good. We weren't out of the car two minutes, when a California Highway Patrol car pulled up next to us. The CHP officer got out. From behind his aviator sunglasses he asked me what happened. I had to explain how I misjudged the curve in the road and hit the center divider.

He looked at me like I was on drugs. But it was obvious to him I wasn't high, and hadn't been using alcohol. He asked for my driver's license, car registration, and insurance. I took them out of my wallet and handed them to him. He asked all of us to stay near my *now-totaled new car* away from the traffic, as he went back to his patrol car and ran my information into his computer.

I was a clean driver with no outstanding tickets or warrants. I thanked the Good Samaritan driver for his concern and he went on his way. I told the CHP officer I had AAA road service. He called us a tow truck. He seemed irritated he couldn't give me a ticket. He didn't see what happened, and neither did the Good Samaritan driver. There aren't any laws, or at least there weren't back then, against accidentally ramming your car into the center divider on the freeway. Maybe he could have given me a ticket for reckless driving, but he had not seen me driving.

A large, flatbed tow truck arrived. The driver, a hulky fella, who looked like he did pro wrestling on the side, put what was left of my car on it. Wendy, Snoopy, and I got into the cab of the tow truck with the driver and drove off. Snoopy had to lie on my lap. I kissed him and let him know everything would be okay. He smiled as usual.

The driver took us to the nearest tow yard that accepted AAA. It was only a few minutes away and I was thankful they were open on Sunday. I signed the paperwork he needed to have signed and thanked him for the lift. He then unloaded my car down onto the dirt, unhooked the tow cable, secured it, and flipped the steel flatbed tilt-tray back into its original position. He got in his truck and drove away.

The tow yard was part of a small automotive junkyard, about an acre lot, with an adjoining repair shop where they fixed cars, and wheeled and dealed in wrecked vehicles like mine. I looked at my new totaled car, lying dead in the dirt. I loved the way it drove. It was my first Toyota and I was hooked. I bought another Camry with the insurance money several weeks later.

I called my cousin, told her what happened, and gave her directions for where to pick us up. It was still morning, so we had plenty of time to make arrangements to get back home. The proprietor of the tow yard, a wiry man in dirty workman coveralls, seemed like an okay guy. I chit-chatted with him about his place of business...my accident...killing time...waiting for my cousin.

Wendy was standing next to me, Snoopy at my side on-leash, when we heard this wild, guttural, cat hissing noise. It wasn't the kind of hissing you hear from your typical domesticated house cat. It had an underlying tone of something seriously ticked-off. From behind a pile of greasy, rusty car parts slowly walked a scrawny, dirty, brown and black cat, and it was not happy.

Snoopy saw him or her and made his "I-want-to-play-puppy-dog-whine," but the whine abruptly stopped as he realized that this cat was not friendly at all. Its wild hissing and stalking-like moves were intended for him. This was the first and only time I had ever seen a *junkyard cat*. Not only was it unafraid of dogs, I got the impression this cat had whipped some serious dog-butt over the years, and was getting ready to attack Snoopy, as it came closer and closer.

I pulled Snoopy behind me the best I could. I tensed up and thought, "If this crazy cat comes anywhere near my dog, I'm going to kick it like a soccer ball." I asked the proprietor if it was his cat. He calmly stated, "Oh, that's Betty. She's not used to seeing dogs around here." *Betty*. Well, you'd better watch yourself, Betty.

I asked if he could please get her away from us while I took Snoopy out of the yard. He yelled, "Go on, Betty! Go on! Get!" Betty hissed her evil hiss one more time, sneered at Snoopy, and slowly exited the way she entered; behind the pile of greasy, rusty car parts. I quickly got Snoopy out of there and we all waited on the street, with me watching out of the corner of my eye for Betty the Junkyard Cat.

-31-

2006: LAS VEGAS AND THE YEAR OF MAJOR CHANGE

In 2005, it seemed banks were giving out home loans to anyone with a pulse. I had never owned a home and neither had Wendy. We had decent assets and our individual credit scores were over 800, which made anyone who handed out loans drool. No reason why we couldn't get a home loan; be homeowners; be part of the so-called American dream. At the end of 2005, we went to Washington Mutual Bank, now JP Morgan Chase Bank, to see if we qualified.

To our surprise, the loan office approved us for slightly over $400,000. That may seem like a lot in some parts of the United States, and in other countries, but in the Greater Los Angeles area in 2005 we would have been lucky to find a crappy two-bedroom condo in a crappy neighborhood with that budget. Many houses had more than doubled in value in a few years. When we had first been married in 2002, we looked at a 1400 square foot house in Burbank listed at $400,000. In 2005, the same house was valued between $700,000 and $800,000. Ludicrous, if you ask me.

Since we couldn't buy a decent house in a good neighborhood, and we wanted to own real estate, we looked at buying income property out-of-state. Arizona seemed to have some good deals at the time. Tri-plex and four-unit apartment buildings were going for $250,000 to $350,000. We looked at properties in Phoenix and Tucson several times, but nothing came to fruition.

On a flight back to Los Angeles from Phoenix, I ran into a guy I hadn't seen in 25 years, a former 80s hunky TV heartthrob, who had dropped out of show business and was now in the mortgage and real estate business. We had worked together on a few episodes of a sitcom. He was a horrific actor, who got by on his good looks, so it was no surprise that he went into a business many former TV actors go into. I'll refer to him as BS, which is more than an accurate set of initials for this conniving, scamming, con artist. BS and I exchanged phone numbers and sort-of reconnected, even though we had not been that good of friends 25 years ago. We were around the same age and seemed to get along fairly well. He was fun to hang out with. At this juncture, I didn't know what he was really like.

During one of our get-togethers, BS was raving about the great home investment opportunities in Las Vegas. He owned a home there, as well as several in Southern California and other parts of the country. He wasn't lying about his homes and business successes, those were real. He said me and my wife should consider buying a home in Las Vegas, that he could get us a loan through his mortgage company, and that he knew real estate people in Las Vegas. BS was much more convincing as a mortgage and real estate person than he had ever been as an actor. If he had been this good on TV, he'd still be in the public consciousness as one of the all-time great actors ever to grace the boob tube.

I was sick of Los Angeles, so his timing was perfect. I had lived and worked in the City of Angels since I was a teenager, never lived anywhere else except Detroit, and Tucson for a few months as a kid. I so desperately wanted to own a home. Many of my friends owned homes, even the woman who cleaned our apartment was a homeowner. She bought her home in the 1980s. It tripled in value, and all she did was clean houses. Maybe I was in the wrong business.

Wendy and I went to Las Vegas to look at houses with a friend of BS's as our real estate agent. This real estate agent, who showed us around for a couple of days, was a tall, geeky man in his late-thirties. His most memorable feature was that his voice had the unpleasant phoniness of a late night infomercial pitchman. One of those, "Hey, how ya doin'? Ain't life beautiful?" type of guys. We were so naïve, we even bought the guy lunch because he was so *nice*. We had no clue how much commission real estate agents were making, or the amount of referral fees people like BS received. Bottom line: we ended up buying a brand-new house in a newly developed area of Southwest Las Vegas called Mountain's Edge from BS's contact. A gorgeous home in a gated community, 2100 square feet, two stories with many top of the line amenities for only $372,000. In Los Angeles it would've been worth well over $1,000,000— easy. It was simply gorgeous.

BS had also moved to Las Vegas as his permanent residence. I thought, great, I'll have at least one person to hang out with. Well, BS barely ever returned my phone calls. His real estate agent friend, who represented us on the sale, wouldn't speak to me unless I had a referral. Turns out, he alone got a full 6 percent commission on our house. It was a brand new home in a new community, and that's what they paid. He split it with BS.

You do the math. We were little pawns and numbers to them. Our feelings were hurt more than anything. BS didn't even say thank you, or take us to lunch. Heck, he should have bought us dinner for a month. The reality was that no one had held a gun to our heads and told us to move. It was just the deceitful tactics and little lies I found out about later that got under my skin. If only they could have been more like dogs, straightforward and honest with everything they were doing, but it wasn't in them. They were more like vultures. On a positive note, we loved our new house. Though, it was going to take a while getting used to living in the desert.

Our move in date was September 6, 2006. We packed up our apartment in Toluca Lake Adjacent. Snoopy sat on the front lawn of our building and watched the movers load their truck for as many hours as it took. He must've followed me up and down the entrance steps 30 or 40 times. He wasn't letting me out of his sight. No one was going to abandon him again. Like humans who've had a bad or traumatic experience as a child and carry it into adulthood, the same goes for dogs.

The move to Las Vegas was smooth. The movers I found on Craigslist did a great job, at a great price. They got it done in one day. When I told BS about them—before he got his referral fee and wouldn't talk to me anymore—he asked for their phone number. I gave it to him. He called and convinced them to bring along his lawn furniture from his Valley home to his Las Vegas home, *on our trip*. The guy had tremendous manipulative powers. He was, hands down, one of the biggest jackasses I have ever dealt with.

Snoopy acclimated to our new Las Vegas home almost instantly. There was no taking a couple of weeks wondering what was going on. He walked through the front door and was like a puppy again; running up and down the stairs, in and out of the rooms, and all around. Melvin was his usual self and immediately acted like he owned the place. The backyard wasn't landscaped yet. It was just a bunch of dirt and weeds, so I rarely let Snoopy go back there—too dusty. His fur seemed to absorb dirt like a dust mop.

Our house was on a cul-de-sac. The name of our new street with our new home was believe it or not...*Cheerful Valley Avenue*. When I first heard the name, it made me chuckle. It sounded like it should be a street name at Disneyland, or an amusement park for little kids. "Boys and girls...Welcome to Cheerful Valley Avenue. Our next stop is Happy-Happy Lane." There were so many new homes and subdivisions being built in the Las Vegas area at the time, the real estate developers must have had a bunch of guys sitting in a room throwing out names and laughing.

We couldn't have asked for better neighbors in our new 'hood. We all moved into our homes around the same time. The best thing about them? Most of them were dog people.

-32-

MORE NEW NEIGHBORS AND THEIR POOCHES

Living next door to us in Las Vegas were Linda and Tom, two fun loving people, who worked in the casinos. Many people in our neighborhood worked for the casinos. What else could I expect in Las Vegas? It would be like living in Detroit and discovering none of your neighbors worked in the auto industry.

Linda was in her sixties; a 20-year plus blackjack dealer, who worked at New York, New York Hotel and Casino on the Las Vegas Strip. When she was younger, she would have given Ann-Margret a run for her money in the looks department. Her partner in crime, Tom, an ex-Vietnam Marine and avid fisherman, managed a series of small casinos for the Boyd Corporation. Casinos like Jokers Wild and Sam's Town, miles away from the strip that cater mostly to locals. Linda, an enormous dog lover, fell in love with Snoopy at first sight. She went completely nuts for him. He was allowed in her home any time. Snoopy liked her, too.

The following Valentine's Day, Tom presented Linda with a gift of love—a purebred Pomeranian puppy. They named him Buzzy. Buzzy would become Snoopy's best dog pal for the remainder of his life. Little Buzz, as I called him, loved him some Snoopy. He looked like he could be Snoopy's half-brother from a different father. They were both from the Spitz family of dogs, Snoopy being part American Eskimo. They looked cute together.

At first, Tom wouldn't let Buzzy near Snoopy and I didn't know why. He'd see me and Snoopy coming toward Buzzy and without a word, he'd quickly take Buzzy inside their house. I later found out he was being overly protective... and a little rude.

Buzzy hadn't been near any full-grown dogs in his young life. He wasn't socialized with dogs, and Tom was scared Snoopy might hurt his little pup. Snoopy convinced him otherwise. One morning, Linda and Tom walked out the front door of their house with Buzzy on-leash. I was outside with Snoopy, on-leash, sitting on our front porch enjoying my yerba mate tea. Snoopy whined when he saw Buzzy, wanting to play. Linda didn't like Tom keeping Buzzy away from Snoopy; she knew he would never hurt him. She let Buzzy off-leash. He ran right for Snoopy and I let him off-leash. They played so well together; it was a joy to watch. Tom realized he was wrong. Little Buzz now had a new big-brother and protector.

Buzzy was a wild little thing, and a lot of fun. He would jump into my arms from the ground, like a Jack Russell terrier. He'd be so happy to see me sometimes; he'd bark and chase himself in a circle. When Buzzy and Snoopy would play in front of our houses, they would have what I call "mark your turf" competitions.

Here's how it went down: Snoopy would pee on the rock lawn. Seconds behind him Buzzy would pee in almost the exact same spot. Snoopy would then pee on a bush. BOOM! Buzzy was right on his butt, peeing behind him near the same spot. Sometimes the little guy would be underneath Snoopy as he peed, wanting to see *exactly* where he was making his mark, and he'd almost get pissed on. Tom would yell at him to, "Get away from there!" Goofy dogs.

Snoopy with his best dog friend, Buzzy the Pomeranian

Kitty-corner from us lived Jackie and Don; a handsome couple in their thirties, and her two kids, four-year-old daughter, Skylar, and ten-year-old son, Harlan. Jackie also worked for a casino. Her job was one I'd never heard of. She was fluent in Spanish and interpreted for wealthy high-rollers, flown in from Spanish speaking countries by the high-end casino she worked for. She'd take them around to gamble and help them spend their money. Her husband Don was a real estate appraiser. Skylar and Harlan loved Snoopy.

I realize I keep saying "so and so loved Snoopy," but it really was true. I'm not some delusional dog owner, who dresses their dog in different outfits every day, hand-feeds them every meal, and thinks their annoying howling is opera singing. Snoopy was truly special. You can look at his picture and see it in his eyes, in his energy, in the way he carried himself—pure love and sweetness on four feet. His effect on people was truly unique.

Don was the proud owner of a five-pound female toy Yorkie named Kiwi. A real cutie with silky straight brown and black hair, always well-groomed. She was about the size of my two fists put together. Yes, I have large fists. It was fun to watch her run across the street to greet Snoopy with her little legs moving so fast. She looked like a dog running in a movie where they sped up the film for comedic effect. She was too small for Snoopy to play with. She was half the size of Melvin. They would usually sniff "hello" and go their separate ways.

Jackie was usually scared of dogs bigger than Kiwi; some sort of childhood fear. Like Tom was scared Snoopy might hurt Buzzy, she was fearful Snoopy might hurt her little daughter. But the fear subsided when she saw how my boy behaved with her kids. His gentle energy won her over.

-33-

THE HEAT, THE NEW PARK, AND LAS VEGAS SNOW

I knew Las Vegas summers could be brutal. I had been there in the past, performing my stand-up comedy routines in the casinos and it got toasty; 100 to 115 degrees in the afternoon, 85 degrees in the early morning shade. I could stomach the heat by swimming and staying indoors. But *living* in that heat, roughly June through September, is not something I'd recommend for humans, let alone anyone with pets, particularly furry dogs. Outdoor cats must feel like they're in kitty hell.

Seniors retire to Las Vegas because of the desert's "dry heat" supposedly being good for your health. This baffles me. Try walking around the block when it's 110 degrees out. You have to drink a lot of water, as if you're gearing up to run a marathon. Touching the steering wheel in your car after it's been sitting in a parking lot for more than an hour is painful, even with tinted windows and an aluminum sunshade for the windshield. The heat is so intense you have to replace your car battery every year-to-two-years, instead of the usual five. Fun in the sun? Yeah, right.

I would talk to people who lived in Nevada for many

years and they would tell me, "Oh, you get used to the heat." I'd say, "Maybe *you* got used to the heat, but I didn't." I was a bit of a hermit before moving to Las Vegas, and suddenly I felt like I was being quarantined to my air-conditioned house several months out of the year.

Poor Snoopy was wearing a thick fur coat all year round. I wasn't about to shave him for the summer to cool him off. From everything I read about Shelties shaving him was not a good idea. His fur could take years to grow back, if it grew back at all. It was my understanding his fur insulated him from the heat *and* the cold. I knew someone who shaved their American Eskimo for the summer, which Snoopy is part. The dog's fur took a good three to five years to grow back. It looked terrible. No way was I doing that to him. His beautiful fur was going to stay beautiful.

To accommodate him during the summer months, I walked him before 8:00 in the morning, when it was anywhere from 70 to 85 degrees. Then again after 11:00 at night when the temperature dropped back down to the same as morning. Though it was wicked-hot in the afternoon, I would also let him out of the house to pee. He would find a shaded area, quickly pee, and then run back inside where it was cool. Snoopy loved being outdoors, but he hated the Vegas heat.

The reason I was very careful with him in hot weather happened on the day of our move to Las Vegas. He had barely peed before we took the four to five hour drive, so I stopped in the small town of Baker, California, about 90 miles south of Las Vegas, for him to take a leak. The town's claim to fame is they have the world's largest thermometer—and it's broken most of the time. Terrific. It would have been nice to know how hot it was that day.

I later found out that Baker is one of the hottest cities on the West Coast. My car didn't have an outside temperature display, so I had no clue. When I let Snoopy out of the car to pee, it was so hot he hopped around on the cement like someone had given him a hot foot in an old silent comedy movie. He quickly hopped over to a nearby patch of burnt grass and peed. He wouldn't move. He stayed there. He liked the little bit of comfort his feet derived from the warm grass. I felt so bad. I carried him back into the car and gave him a biscuit. I examined the bottom of his feet. They were slightly hot to the touch. Thankfully, they weren't blistered.

After eighteen months of living in Las Vegas, a beautiful 24-acre community park opened, less than one mile from our house. It was called Mountain's Edge Exploration Park. It had several acres of newly-planted green grass, a stretch of sidewalk curving around the park for walking or running, and cement picnic tables and benches with nearby brick barbecues. It also had a children's section with swings, slides, and climbing bars. The children's slide didn't have stairs like Verdugo Park had in Burbank, so Snoopy wasn't able to climb up it. There were also restrooms, a parking lot, and security guards on bicycles, who wore dark blue shirts with the word SECURITY emblazoned in bright yellow across the chest and back.

Everything was new and looked good. The only drawback; there were signs placed every fifty yards warning you that you had to keep your dog on a leash. Snoopy missed the grass and parks I used to take him to in California. He loved running, playing, and dumping on grass. Living in the desert with a landscaped rock lawn in front of our house and irrigated trees and bushes didn't seem very natural.

Here we had this great, man-made park with beautiful grass, and I had to keep Snoopy on-leash? No way, José! The security guards weren't cops. They couldn't write me a ticket for having him off-leash. I knew leash laws were there to prevent the possibility of dog bites, attacks, and whatnot. Snoopy wasn't going to bite anyone, and there weren't any wild Pit Bulls roaming through the park. Whatever justification I gave myself, I was willing to *skirt the leash law* for a few minutes. I wanted to let my boy run free. It had been a while.

The first time I brought Snoopy to the new park and he saw the grass, his eyes, nose, and ears perked up like he was a puppy again, and he was now eleven years-young. We stood at the edge of the grass, several acres in front of us. I looked around. No security guards in site. Snoopy whined and tugged at his leash, telling me he wanted to frolic through it. I unhooked his leash from his collar. He ran several yards, kicked his hind legs on the ground, causing blades of grass to fly into the air behind him, and then took off running. I cheered him on, "Go, Snoopy, go! Go, Snoopy, go!" He was having a grand time.

I gained instant joy from his enthusiasm. Big smiles on both of our faces. Then he did something I'd never seen him do before. He started running with his nose to the ground, smelling everything in his path. It looked funny. He looked like a dog lawnmower, mowing grass with no grass being cut. He was so excited, he didn't want to miss any smells in this magical new place I had brought him to. Who knew when he might come here again?

A few other dog owners at the park looked at my boy and smiled. I let Snoopy run for several minutes, until I noticed, about 50 yards away, a security guard riding his bicycle in our direction. Better get Snoopy back on-leash. I gave a command, "Snoopy, come! Snoopy, come here!" I flicked the chrome plated pin within the hook on his leash. It made a loud "ping" noise. That was the signal I used to let him know he was going back on-leash, along with me yelling at him to bring his *butt over here.* He obliged and we avoided having to deal with the security guard.

Another fun thing I would do with Snoopy at the new park was fly my kite. To make our playtime hassle free, I would avoid the security guards by bringing Snoopy there at 8:00 in the morning or earlier. They started work at 9:00.

My kite was nylon, and put together with plastic tubing and latches; a far cry from the paper and wood kites of my youth. Though synthetic, it was still a blast to let it go and watch the wind take it. I held the string tight, let out a little at a time, and it moved higher and higher toward the sky. But the best part was having my boy Snoopy with me.

For some unknown reason he loved to chase my kite just like he loved chasing a motorized toy truck. My kite was black with big white shark teeth drawn on the front. I didn't buy it because I liked sharks; I bought it because it was the cheapest one I could find with a decent wingspan.

Snoopy would bark and run after it with the wind blowing his fur all around. His eyes would follow the kite sailing upward as I ran to maneuver it and get it as high as the string would take it. It wasn't quite as if Snoopy was trying to jump into the air to get it, although, it would have been *cool beans* if he had flown after it like a super dog in a cartoon or comic strip. No, Snoopy would merely look up, watch the kite, and run and bark in whatever direction it moved.

Maybe he chased it because of its size, or movement, which seems like a possible explanation. Doctors, scientists, and so-called animal experts will tell you what *they believe* goes on with your animal's behavior, yet they really don't know for certain. Just like there's so much unexplained human behavior, there's more unexplained dog behavior.

I say just enjoy the beauty of your pooch, and his or her harmless and fun behaviors, without trying to analyze it too much. If your dog likes chasing kites or motorized toys, or whatever, have fun watching them have fun. Unless they have a fascination with chasing cars. Then it's best to keep them on-leash when moving vehicles are present.

As time went on, I was beginning to despise Las Vegas and questioned why we moved there in the first place. We couldn't move back to California right away even if we wanted to. We were on the hook with a mortgage that wasn't pretty. According to some reports I read, from around 2008 to 2012 Las Vegas had seven times more foreclosures than any other city in the United States. Being a homeowner was sucking big-time.

Another fun time with Snoopy was when it snowed in Las Vegas. It snowed in Las Vegas? In the desert? Yes it did. It snowed every several years or so. I remember performing in Las Vegas during Christmas week of 1988, and it snowed several inches.

Driving in snow on the 15 freeway south out of Las Vegas on my way back to Los Angeles was something I will never forget. The morning traffic was light, but it was moving *soooo* slow. I learned to drive in snow and ice in

Detroit, when I was fifteen. No big deal. I had a blast driving through it until the snow was gone. It ended after about twenty miles. All of a sudden it just stopped, like the clouds had a planned cutoff point. Snow coming down then, BAM! No snow. I should have taken a picture.

I did take pictures in mid-December of 2008 when it snowed hard in Las Vegas...well, hard for Las Vegas; about eight inches. Seeing snow on our rock lawn was weird. I sure as heck couldn't lie down on it and make snow angels without some serious body bruises. I was able to make a snowman and I have pictures to prove it. I rolled three snowballs along our driveway and down the street, until they became three giant snowballs and built Mr. Snowman in front of our house. I gave him eyes and a smile made out of rocks and a carrot for a nose. I felt like a little boy again.

Snoopy loved the snow, like he had in Chicago, only there were no silver squirrels for him to chase, which was fine with me. I watched him walk and run around the cul-de-sac as snow fell on his fur, coating him with what looked like a shiny white frost. He looked so pretty—my snow dog. It was so cold, white breath came out of his mouth and nostrils. I took several pictures of him and luck was on my side. I captured one shot of him standing tall and proud with white breath coming out of his nostrils. It looks like he's blowing smoke. It's a great shot. Of the hundreds of pictures I took of him over the years, it's one of my favorites.

Snoopy in the Las Vegas Snow

-34-

2009: OLD AGE ARRIVES

Summer 2009. Snoopy began to show signs of aging. He was around twelve years-old and arthritis was creeping into his joints. He could no longer climb up the stairs to the second floor in our home. I missed his comforting presence in my office, and him lying near our bed at night. His suffering disturbed me, but I had to look at the positive.

Many breeds show signs of arthritis much earlier in life. Getting arthritis at such a late age may have been due to the fact I fed him chewable glucosamine chondroitin tablets from six years-old on. Snoopy could still run and walk like always, but his hind legs no longer had the flexibility to move up stairs. It was painful for him. Sometimes I would carry him to the second floor to be with me.

Oddly enough, he had little problem going *down* the stairs on his own. But as time went on, he could only go down the stairs on his own if he were revved up from a twenty or 30 minute bath, where warm water pulsated against his body and his blood was flowing. It made him run like a pup. He'd run along the carpeted hallway and down the stairs to the first floor, like he had many times before. I wish I could have relieved him of his pain like that all the time. It made both of us smile.

Snoopy at age twelve...still smiling and still handsome

One day, in December 2009, when I touched Snoopy's right front leg, it caused him pain. From the outside it looked fine. I examined it and his paw more closely. He hadn't stepped on a nail, or had any type of wound I could see. I increased his dosage of glucosamine and chondroitin and MSM supplements. It didn't help. Time for a visit to a Las Vegas vet. I found one close to our house that opened in 2008. I looked at the vet's Curriculum Vitae online. She hadn't been practicing long, but seemed adequate. I mean we weren't talking brain surgery here; my boy had a sore leg.

We arrived at the vet's office, did the usual routine of filling out paperwork, and waited for several minutes until my name was called. The vet greeted me and Snoopy and we followed her into an exam room. She was a thin, attractive woman in her early-thirties, and seemed quite knowledgeable. She was up-to-date on the latest medical technologies in veterinary medicine. Her office was equipped with state-of-the-art testing gear to take Snoopy's vitals.

He particularly disliked what I'll call an "electronic anal probe" a.k.a., a digital rectal thermometer. Why did they have to stick this thing up my dog's sphincter and make him uncomfortable? With all the miracle medical devices nowadays why hasn't someone created an unbreakable thermometer a dog can bite down on to get a temperature reading?

Snoopy's vitals were good. The vet wanted to do full blood work on him, which I refused. As if his cholesterol was bad. No wonder they put a thermometer up your dog's butt, it's a metaphor for them attempting to charge you up the butt, with as many tests as they can talk you into under the guise of it being in the best interest of your four-legged friend.

The vet couldn't find anything wrong from her very-thorough physical exam, except that he had arthritis in his hind legs and his right front leg hurt him if you touched it, and I had known that walking in. To dig a little deeper, I opted for an x-ray. Her price of ninety bucks seemed fair. In a vet's office, I would always ask the price of each test or additional procedure they wanted to do before committing. If you don't, you might pay hundreds of extra dollars, or more, for unnecessary treatment.

Up Snoopy went on the cold medal table for his x-ray. The vet was okay with me helping place his leg in the correct position. He had to be twisted like a pretzel and muzzled in order for the x-ray machine to get the needed images. Poor baby. If the vet or one of her assistants had done it without me Snoopy would not have been as cooperative.

It took all of one minute. I carried him off the table and removed the muzzle. He smiled and wagged his tail.

I gave him a biscuit. He knew the worst was over. The vet looked over the x-ray images on her computer. She found nothing out of the ordinary. No sign of arthritis in his front leg whatsoever. No tumor, no strange clot or bump... nothing. That was a relief, but what the heck was causing his condition? Why was he acting this way? What was causing the pain in his front right leg? Something was wrong and I had no clear answers, which was very frustrating.

I asked for a copy of the x-rays for my records. The vet burned them onto a CD and I put it in my notebook. Our visit was done. I thanked her and paid my bill to the vet assistant, seated behind the counter near the front entrance. She printed out a receipt, handed it to me, and asked if I wanted to schedule a follow-up visit. I declined. I said goodbye and me and Snoopy were out the door.

Like the vet who wanted to prescribe Snoopy Prozac, I didn't get a good feeling from this vet. It wasn't her words or actions; in fact she seemed genuine and very well-trained. But my gut told me not to take Snoopy back to see her...and I listened to my gut.

-35-

2010: A CHALLENGING YEAR

I was very unhappy living in Las Vegas and financially it was a major pain. Our beautiful home, bought in September 2006, was now worth less than half of what we had paid. A second income property we had acquired at the end of 2008 was losing its value at an alarming rate. Like many throughout the country, and the world, we were losing our home and investment. We wanted out. We were done with Las Vegas.

The banks wouldn't negotiate. They wouldn't give us loan modifications, or allow our short sales to go through. We had been in the process of doing short sales for both properties for several months. After jerking Wendy, me, and our real estate agents around, they basically said in a form letter, "Sorry, we're foreclosing!" Wendy and I were feeling the stress of the housing crisis. If there were an upside, some might consider not having to pay two mortgages for a while an upside. But it wasn't. In our credit conscious world we paid dearly by having two foreclosures on our credit reports.

Work was slow, and when it did come I had to make trips to Los Angeles, mostly for voice work on video games.

I didn't mind the drive. I was beginning to miss the city I had grown sick-of and left four years earlier to have the so-called American dream of owning a home. Some dream.

Back to Snoopy. His front right leg was getting worse. Maybe it was just part of him getting older. I didn't know. His symptoms became very odd. He could walk on his front legs, no problem, but if I put my hand anywhere near his right front leg, he would snap at it, as though he were going to bite me. It seemed like some sort of weird reflex reaction. I really didn't know what it was. It was a mystery. I probably could have taken him to a dozen vets and they wouldn't have found anything.

As the weeks passed, it seemed as if the arthritis in his hind legs was also getting worse. When I'd take him for a walk, he'd linger behind me at a snail's pace just like the old black Lab back in Burbank. I'd pull hard on his leash and he'd walk ahead for several yards wanting ever-so-much to be his younger self and please his master. Then he'd fall back behind me. I'd yell, "C'mon Snoopy, let's go!" and run, trying to get him to follow after me. I felt if I could get his blood flowing, like when he received a bath, he would move more easily. I wanted him to be pain-free. If I could have taken his pain into my body to relieve his hurt, I would have done it in a femtosecond. My heart was breaking. It breaks again as I write this.

As time went on, Snoopy's symptoms became even odder. At one point, if I petted any part of him, he would snap at me, as if touching his fur caused him pain. Not only was this bizarre, but it was physically impossible. Dog fur doesn't have nerve-endings. The way I first noticed it...was with a stranger.

Early one morning, I was walking Snoopy around the block. A cute little boy who I'd never seen before, about four or five, with bangs and dressed as if his parents just got him ready for school, was standing in front of his house. He saw us walking by and was excited to see Snoopy. He asked if he could pet him. I said okay, but be gentle and pet him nice. At this point Snoopy was slowed to a stop. The boy reached out his hand. He softly petted the top of Snoopy's head in a sweet curious manner like only a small boy can. SNAP! Snoopy's head quickly turned in the direction of the boy as his jaws snapped together, making an alarming sound of teeth hitting teeth. It scared the boy, and it scared me even more. I jerked Snoopy's leash, moving his head away from the young boy.

I could see the boy was on the verge of tears. He made a slight whimpering sound. The sound you hear right before a small child breaks out in a cry. I stopped it cold by saying, "No, no, don't worry, don't be upset. My doggie's not feeling well. I better take him home. Okay?" He said, "Okay," and I got Snoopy out of there as fast as I could. In the coming months his snapping got so bad that I was the only one who could get close to him without him being muzzled.

-36-

MORE CHALLENGES

Summer 2010. As far as I could tell, Snoopy's arthritis remained about the same. I wished he could communicate about his pain. Answer questions like, "Where does it hurt?" "Is it a sharp or a dull pain?" "Are the supplements helping?" How does anyone know, how one's pet or pets *really* feel? Only a dog's communication of love is ever-present. My poor, poor Snoopy. Poor animals in general. They suffer in silence.

Putting Snoopy's dog collar on without having him snap at me became a game. I had to do it very fast. I'd hold it outstretched with both hands underneath his neck. This way he didn't know where my hands were going. Then I'd quickly wrap it around his neck and snap the ends together. Part of him wanted his collar on; he knew we were going outside for a walk. He still loved being outdoors. He had no problem with me attaching his leash to the collar.

The groomer I used to take Snoopy to from time to time refused to groom him. The snapping was something they didn't want to deal with. There were issues of safety as well as insurance. They were doing what was best for my dog and their employees. They were saddened by his condition.

I had to muzzle him to give him a bath. I knew it caused him discomfort, but thankfully I only did it every six weeks or so, and I would do it as quickly as possible. He couldn't pant very well with the muzzle on while being bathed.

I decided to take Snoopy to another vet on the north side of town, who came recommended by my neighbor, Linda. Plus, every person who reviewed him on various websites sang his praises. It was a pain driving twenty-plus miles in the Las Vegas summer heat, but anything for my boy. In my air conditioned car it was always hotter in the backseat where Snoopy would lie. He would have to endure it, and so would I.

Putting him in the car was an ordeal. He no longer had the strength in his legs to jump into the car like he had for many years. I purchased a doggie ramp for him to walk up. I'd lay one end on the edge of the backseat with the door open. The other end would rest on the ground on about a 30-degree angle. Snoopy was supposed to walk up it and get in the car. For some reason he did not like the ramp. He wouldn't go near it. I had to put the muzzle on him, then place him in the backseat, take the muzzle off for the drive, and put it back on when we arrived at the vet's office so I could get him out of the car. Then I'd have to take it off again inside the vet's office, so he could examine him.

The vet was in his late-fifties. He had been practicing a good twenty years and had a confidence I hadn't seen since Snoopy's first vet, Dr. Altman. I liked and trusted the guy for the most part. Examining Snoopy without a muzzle lasted all of five seconds. He snapped at the vet and back on it went. The vet couldn't figure out the cause of Snoopy's snapping. His vitals were good. No fever, heart and lungs were good, ears and eyes seemed okay.

He x-rayed Snoopy from the waist down and the results were what I assumed—severe arthritis. He prescribed an arthritis medication called Deramaxx. I agreed to it. At this point, anything holistic or natural was not going to help my boy. He needed something stronger. He was thirteen years old and had never needed so-called traditional medication until now, which in itself was a miracle of sorts. The vet sold me the few remaining pills of Deramaxx he had in the office. They would last several days. I then ordered a three month supply online at 1-800-PetMeds, where it was cheaper.

The pills were chewable, liver-flavored. Snoopy ate them like candy. Through his pain and getting older, his appetite remained excellent like it always had. He still scarfed his food down like he was a pup. His snapping condition puzzled me and the vet. What was *this*? After extensive research online, I still couldn't find anything.

Another habit Snoopy developed during this time was crapping in the house. He had no idea he was doing it. It was like he wasn't in control of his senses down there. He would crap on the carpet, the tile, wherever. At first I got upset and would yell at him. But I soon realized it was like he was almost reverting back to puppyhood. Not knowing where it was okay, or not okay, to go to the bathroom until he had been trained otherwise. Sort of like when old person mentally reverts back to acting like a little kid again.

Maybe that theory is bull. Maybe when you get older you realize many things in life are bull. That it's all been bull and you act like a kid again, or a ticked off kid, because you finally found the answers you were looking for about life and happiness, and they didn't mean a whole lot. You realize you should have simply had a good time, as if you were a carefree child. George Bernard Shaw said, "Youth is wasted on the young."

Snoopy crapping around the house wasn't too bad. The dry dog food I fed him caused his poop to come out extremely firm. I'd pick it up with a napkin and spray where he pooped with white vinegar and water to disinfect the area. It was so sad to see him like this. My heart was breaking day-by-day, yet he smiled and seemed happy through it all.

That's one of the reasons I love him, and dogs in general. They are pure love and nothing means more than loving their master—no matter what they're going through, even to the end. From time-to-time over the years, I'd accidentally stepped on Snoopy's paw or tail when I didn't see him lying on the floor. He'd cry or whine in pain for a moment as I was saying, "Sorry, sorry, sorry!" and comforting him. Within a second or so, he'd lick my hand or leg with a kiss of forgiveness. If I could have on tenth, one thirtieth, one one-hundredth of that in me, I'd be a much better person.

-37-

THE DIAGNOSIS

I think the arthritis medication might have helped a little. Snoopy's condition wasn't getting any worse. It may have stabilized it. I still walked him around the block in our neighborhood and he continued to move slowly behind me. I'd let him off-leash in front of the house a few times a day so he could pee. Thankfully he never peed in the house. He still had excellent control of his bladder.

In addition I gave him other supplements to *try* and give him more relief. Stuff like acetyl-l-carnitine, a supplement used to improve brain function; DMG, a.k.a., dimethylglycine, an amino acid to help boost the immune system, and water soluble silver, also for his immune system. Maybe they helped, I don't know. It was so hard to tell. I didn't want to face the fact he was nearing the end of his life.

Thursday, November 3, 2010 is a day I will never forget. It is ingrained in my brain. It had been fifteen weeks since Snoopy was examined by the vet on the north side of town. I fed him his breakfast of dry food, supplements, and the Deramaxx pill. He finished, walked a few feet, looked up at me and smiled. Then in the flash of a second, he lost his balance.

His hind legs fell out from underneath him. His stomach hit the stone tile floor and he couldn't get up. He tried his best, but had no control over those muscles. He was spread out like an animal rug, shaking and moving, trying to get up. It was disturbing. I heard his nails scratch against the stone tile, as he tried again and again to get up. *I panicked.*

"Snoopy, what's wrong? Snoopy! Snoopy!"

Snoopy! I reached to pick him up and the snapping started. There was no way I could get a muzzle on him in this situation. He couldn't get up and he was snapping at me as I attempted to move him into the living room, where his legs would have a better chance of gripping the plush Berber carpet, enabling him to stand.

I sat down on the floor behind him with my hands at my sides, pressing down on the tile for balance, and I pushed his butt with my feet. I tried to slide him toward the living room about ten feet away, as he repeatedly snapped, sneered and then *growled ferociously* at me. It was as if he were possessed by something other than himself. I had never seen him like this. His behavior scared me. At that moment in time...he was not my dog.

It's hard to describe in words. It's a moment in both our lives I'd rather not have happened. I kept pushing him with my feet as he slid on the tile, growling and snapping. After a few seconds he made it onto the carpet. Once on it he regained his balance on all fours and wandered around as though nothing had happened. He was his sweet self again. I was happy he was off the tile, but I knew something just took place that was telling me there was something *very seriously* wrong with him.

I immediately called the vet's office on the north side

of town. I told the assistant who answered the phone what happened. That it was an emergency and I needed to bring Snoopy in right away. She could hear the panic in my voice and told me to come in A.S.A.P. I did my usual routine with the muzzle, got Snoopy in the car, and it was off to the vet's office once again. I was glad it was November and not very hot outside. Snoopy would be more comfortable on the drive.

The vet examined him—his vitals were good, like always. He said he honestly didn't know what was going on with Snoopy; that his issues were beyond his level of expertise. He suggested I take him immediately to the Las Vegas Veterinary Referral Center. They were experts in advanced animal diagnostics. The Las Vegas Veterinary Referral Center? What kind of place was this?

It was 8:30 in the morning. The vet had his assistant call them and make an appointment. The earliest they could see Snoopy was 11:30. I asked if we could be seen sooner. The answer was no. 11:30 it would have to be.

I thanked the vet, paid the examination fee, and left. I wasn't going home. I drove around, killed time, whatever. I needed answers and I wanted them immediately. I was completely stressed out. I'm stressed out remembering it and writing about it. Snoopy was calm, smiling as usual in the backseat of the car, happy to be outside and riding with his master. Other than wandering around a thrift store for a few minutes looking to buy stuff I didn't need, I can't remember much of anything else I did in those three hours until our appointment.

11:30 that morning. Snoopy and I arrived at the Las Vegas Veterinary Referral Center. I didn't like the place, although they served a useful purpose. It was an animal hospital that worked exclusively on referral from other vets. It was primarily for animals on the verge of dying, and the doctors were highly qualified to diagnose any type of advanced or critical disease.

I parked my car as close as I could to the front entrance in the adjoining parking lot. I exited and opened the rear passenger door. Snoopy was lying in the backseat, smiling like always. I told him I loved him and once again put the muzzle on him. I picked him up, slammed the car door shut with my foot, and proceeded to carry him inside. An elderly couple was leaving and opened the door for us. They gave us a sad look upon seeing my dog like this. I thanked them for opening the door.

People waiting in the lobby with their pets were a site I'd rather have not seen. Everyone had a pet in dire straits. I saw a Pug wrapped in a blanket, its head twitching uncontrollably while his owner held him in his arms. A cat was in a cage looking half-dead. Various breeds of dogs lay at their owners' feet in various stages of advanced disease. It's too painful to try and remember more. What a depressing place.

The vet on the north side of town had sent Snoopy's medical records via fax. I checked in at the front desk, filled out my name and address on a form, and signed another form. Then Snoopy and I were sent into an examination room to wait for a doctor. This examination room was rather large, fifteen feet by fifteen feet, or more. I took Snoopy's muzzle off him so he could breathe better. Veterinarian assistants kept coming into the room every ten minutes or so, telling me it would be another few minutes before we saw the doctor; we waited for 45 minutes.

We saw two doctors, a man and a woman. The woman was first to examine Snoopy. She was friendly and professional. I muzzled Snoopy once again and she did a preliminary exam, looking into his eyes with a light, feeling around his body for lumps, and writing her findings on a chart. She left the room and I removed the muzzle. Several minutes later, the male doctor came in. He was in his late-thirties, British or Australian, I can't remember. His demeanor was calm and confident. He had a good way about him. It made me relax a little.

I answered his questions about Snoopy. What happened, his age, habits, health, and whatnot. He started to examine him and the snapping started. He took the muzzle and attempted to put on it on him. I could see he was scared of getting bit so I said, "Better let me do that." I had gotten pretty good at putting it on and had him muzzled in about three seconds. The doctor smiled and joked that I should get a job there. No way.

He also examined Snoopy with his hands, the light in his eyes, his ears, and listened to inside of his body with a stethoscope. He was very thorough. When he finished, he told me he was almost certain the symptoms of Snoopy's snapping, the way he moved and his interactions, were *neurological* problems. Most likely...he had a brain tumor. I remained calm as I could, my eyes instantly watering. I didn't break out in a pool of tears and hysterical crying. I asked questions and he answered them intelligently and with the utmost respect for both of us.

It was obvious this guy had been around and was one smart fellow. My boy's brain was malfunctioning. With a test, they could look inside his head—a doggy brain scan. He would have to be put under anesthesia. I don't remember much more regarding other tests they wanted to do, because inside, part of me was so completely upset I wanted to breakdown right then and there. I was an emotional wreck.

I knew putting a thirteen-and-a-half year-old dog under anesthesia was not a good thing. Some don't survive that. I could lose him from that alone. I asked the doctor if they found a brain tumor and it was operable and they got it out, would he live another few years and be a happy, healthy guy? If they could guarantee that, I didn't care what it cost, I would do it. The answer to my question was a big fat, "There are no guarantees." He then said dogs of Snoopy's breed, or mixed breed, live an average of twelve to twelve-and-a-half years. He'd had a long life. I liked what he said, though I didn't want to hear it. He was right. The last year or so had been very rough on Snoopy, and he had been getting worse and worse during that time.

I asked how much the doggy brain scan, or whatever it was called, would cost. It was roughly $2400. He then prescribed a different pain medication called Tramadol, to ease Snoopy's arthritis and help him walk a little better. Maybe it could ease his pain. Then I asked a question I never wanted to hear coming from my lips. *How much longer does he have?* The specialist said it could be a week, two weeks, even six months or more.

I shook his hand and thanked him for his diagnosis. There wasn't much else he could tell me and I had heard enough. He knew, and now I knew, the reality of the situation. I could stop lying to myself that Snoopy was going to live a lot longer. It was too painful to stop lying, but I had to. What about Snoopy's pain? He suffered so much for so long and yet I wanted him to live forever. Was I being selfish? Insensitive? I didn't know.

I put Snoopy back in the car then went to the front desk to pay my bill for the visit. The young lady at the counter, possibly a college student, asked if I wanted to schedule a surgery. She said there were two options; one for $2,250 and one for $2,400. I calmly said, "No, thank you." I realized the place was also in the business of making money, lots of money, and she was merely doing her job. I paid the fee for the office visit and a starter pack of the Tramadol arthritis medication.

Out of curiosity, I asked the young lady how she could work there, having to look at dying animals day after day. She calmly replied, "Oh, you get used to it after a while." Someone has to have her job. I thanked her, said goodbye, and left never wanting to see that place again...and I didn't.

-38-

HOPE AND PLANNING

I started Snoopy on the new arthritis medication right away. In 48 hours it seemed to make a difference for the better. The spring in his step was slightly improved. He moved a bit quicker when I called him. At this point he only answered to me, not Wendy, and not anyone who saw him. When his dog buddy Buzzy came by to visit, Snoopy acknowledged him with a sniff, but they didn't play like they normally did. If Little Buzz moved too close to his body, it irritated him, and he would snap and growl at him. Then Snoopy would lose interest and wander around the front of our house.

So many questions and thoughts crossed my mind. How could he have brain damage? I fed him the best dog food, the best supplements, and filtered water his whole life. Was it simply old age? Not every dog gets neurological disorders. At least I didn't have to have him suffer with an operation and be cut open.

I've benefited from holistic and alternative medicine my entire adult life, and I did my best to carry it into Snoopy's life. I tried to look for some sort of bright side in all of this, but I was dying inside. I couldn't sleep. I wanted to spend every waking moment with Snoopy. It was sad I could no longer hold him, pet him, comb out his beautiful coat every week like I used to. No more playing. But he would still come to me the best he could when I called him, and his appetite remained strong. A pig dog always.

I was being very optimistic about the newly prescribed medication. I went online and ordered a three month supply from 1-800-PetMeds. I had a good conversation about Snoopy with the person who took the order, and had high hopes for this medication relieving his pain. That hope didn't last long.

The next morning I could see the medication wasn't really working. It was more of me *wanting* it to work. It was all in my mind. Snoopy wasn't getting any relief. The reality was that he was getting worse and worse. I'd let him outside to pee and I'd have to practically push him out the door. Our front porch had only one step, it was eight inches high, and he couldn't climb up it. He would wander around our driveway, not knowing where he was. After he'd pee, to get him back in the house, I'd have to push him up the step while he snapped at me.

The love of my life was losing his mind. I cried a lot. I may be a strong-willed person when it comes to work, relationships, and life in general, but when it came to my Snoopy being hurt, or in any discomfort, I could not take it. A part of me was dying along with him. Simply writing these words has me in tears and my heart still aches.

I called back 1-800-PetMeds and canceled Snoopy's new medication order. I was practically in tears while talking to the person who answered the phone. I did what I had to do to remain strong during this time. To do what was best for my boy. I researched various pet cemeteries, cremation, and euthanization services around town and made inquiries.

While online, I found the only mobile veterinarian in Las Vegas. I got a good vibe, for lack of better words, from her webpage and listing. She also did in-home euthanizations. If Snoopy's life was going to end, I wanted it to end at home, where he'd be more comfortable. Not on a cold metal table in a vet's office.

I mustered up the courage and called the vet. She had been a practicing veterinarian for fifteen years, and the type of person who wasn't into her work only for the money. She truly believed she was providing a necessary service. We talked for about 45 minutes. I told her all about my Snoopy, his current condition and demeanor. We talked about end-of-life animal issues. She made some very good points, though I can't remember much of it now...my mind goes blank about some of this. It hurts too much. The bottom line: after our conversation I made arrangements for her to come over the following morning, Saturday, November 13th at 9:00, to euthanize Snoopy. It was time. Time I was not looking forward to.

If it were up to me, I would have preferred Snoopy outlive me. I wished and dreamed for a miracle cure that could make him like a puppy again. But that was one wish and one dream that would never come true.

I decided to have Snoopy cremated. At least part of him would always be with me. I made arrangements with a local pet crematorium to pick him up after he was gone. Wendy, Melvin, and I were moving back to Los Angeles, permanently. The plan had been in the works for a few months. I couldn't wait to get out of Las Vegas. I had hoped Snoopy would have been able to move back to sunny California, but that was no longer possible.

Part of me was relieved, I was making this decision to *help* my best friend. Another part was tortured to no end. I was having *the one* I loved more than anything in the world; *the one* I would have done anything for; *the one* who truly loves me unconditionally...killed. It was not a pleasant thought.

I could use the term "put to sleep," but I don't like it. It's not sleep. Sleep you wake up from and you usually wake up refreshed to start your day. This was the right thing to do, but I still to this day look at it as killing, or murder, and it still pains me. Who am I to take an animal's life? Especially the one I love. Sure, it happens all the time. Thousands of dogs die every day in shelters across America, and countless others from abuse and neglect. I don't care to research the exact statistics on this issue. It's too depressing. I was allowing a necessary, but brutal act. I don't condone the killing of any animals, and I do my part by not eating, wearing, or using products made from them.

I've been through various stages of healthy eating. I was a vegan for seven years and then went back to eating fish. Experimented with raw foods, eating raw eggs and cheese, but now I'm back to being a vegan once again. As I get older I seem to be more sensitive to things around me, especially the things I eat. Plus, I love animals too much to ever eat them again. I'm not wacky about it, like I was in my earlier years, where I was so stressed out about what was in the food I was consuming that I was a nervous wreck. I'm more relaxed and educated about my food choices, and their effect on me and the world.

In various parts of the world, *dogs are food.* If someone who consumes dogs as food were to read this book, they would think I was certifiably crazy. It would be like me reading a book about a guy and his love for his *pet fly,* and how it's passing left him devastated. I would think the guy was out of his mind.

Back to Snoopy. I informed Wendy about my decision. It was a tear-fest all through the night. I also told my next-door neighbors, Linda and Tom. They had cared for Snoopy on many occasions when Wendy and I went out of town, and I did the same for Little Buzz. They, too, had seen Snoopy's deterioration over the past year, and especially over the past few months. Linda, who felt a special bond with Snoopy, said goodbye to him, though at this point, I don't think he knew what was going on.

The past few weeks, I hadn't slept or eaten much and I lost 20 pounds, which made me thinner than I already was. I ran into an acquaintance, who hadn't seen me in a while. She commented on my weight loss and asked how I did it. I told her I was on the, *"Too stressed-out to eat, have your dog killed, lose your houses to foreclosure diet,"* but I don't recommend it.

-39-

THE LAST DAY.
GOODBYE, MY FRIEND.

Saturday, November 13, 2010. The arrangements were set. The vet was coming over at 9:00 in the morning to do the deed. The man from the pet cremation service would be there as well. The vet instructed me to lay a sheet of plastic on the floor underneath a blanket where she would give Snoopy the fatal shot, to catch any bodily fluids he might lose after he passed. Snoopy's condition was worse. He would wander around the living room and kitchen not knowing where he was. His hind legs seemed even weaker. It would literally hurt my eyes to see at him like that. He would still come to me and smile the best he could when I would call him. I still couldn't pet or stroke his fur which remained as soft and colorful as it had in his youth.

The day before, I had gone to Whole Foods Market and bought him his last meal; a half pound of raw organic ground beef, raised without antibiotics or hormones, and raw organic eggs. He loved raw eggs, which I gave him from time to time. Around 7:00 that morning, I gave him a quarter pound of the raw beef and one raw egg. It was gone in seconds. I was happy to see him enjoy it so much.

191

Time felt dreamlike. I was about to lose the best friend I had ever had and would never see him again, and it would be because of my doing. I knew I was doing the right thing, but my mind kept telling me over and over, I was having the one I loved more than anything, killed.

Around 8:45, the vet arrived. I was waiting on the front porch when she pulled up in her little red Toyota pickup truck. She was in her mid-to-late forties. Her energy was kind even though she dealt in death. She had a sort of hippy-ish look, and a gentle way of explaining things. Snoopy was wandering around the driveway, smelling some of the last smells his beautiful nose would ever know. The vet wanted cash up front. No problem. She was apologetic about asking for it, stating in the past, she had been written bad checks for her services. Anyone who'd write a bad check to a vet who was helping them and their pet in a situation like this was a real lowlife. Anyhow, I paid the lady in cash and got a receipt.

She removed her equipment from her pickup. It was stored in a blue, hard-plastic case with various compartments and drawers with a handle on top, like a tool box. She observed Snoopy on the driveway. Like many others who crossed his path throughout his life, her first words were, "He's very pretty." Till the end, a beautiful boy. She said she could tell by the way he was moving there were definitely neurological problems. She reassured me I was doing the right thing; at his stage, he could possibly go into painful convulsions, which would have been even worse. Her words comforted me for the time being. Snoopy barely noticed her existence. The old Snoopy would have greeted her—tail wagging, checking out her truck, and everything she was doing. But those days were gone.

While we were talking, the man from the cremation service pulled up in a small white van with his company's name on the doors. He had the look of a brawny Irishman from the Midwest. He was in his forties with thinning hair and a calming presence. I instructed him to park curbside in front of the house. He too was kind, like he had been on the phone. He truly sympathized with my situation. He said he would wait outside while the vet did the euthanization. I would let him know when it was over. It takes a special kind of person to provide these types of services. Dealing with death is not pleasant for most. These two people helped make this dreadful day a little easier.

Wendy came outside for a moment. I introduced her to the vet and she went back inside. I maneuvered Snoopy into the house for the last time, pushing him up the one brick step while he snapped at me. There was no turning back. The vet explained the procedure. One shot to relax him so he would feel no pain, then the second shot—the lethal shot—to stop his heart. Oh, am I sick right now writing this.

I had laid a thick piece of plastic on the carpet, the kind painters use. On top of it, I had laid Snoopy's favorite blanket. I took the remaining beef and another raw egg from the fridge and put it in his bowl. He would be preoccupied with eating when the vet administered the first shot. Not only was it mentally hard for me to say goodbye, but physically it was even harder. Of the thousands of hugs I had given him over the years, the last one had to be done when he was unconscious. At least he would he pain free.

I placed the bowl of food on the blanket and he went right to it. I grabbed him by the collar and the vet administered the first shot into the scruff of his neck. In a matter of seconds, his body went limp. I pushed the bowl of food aside and I could hug my baby once again. The vet told me and Wendy to say goodbye before she gave him the final and fatal shot. We both cried and held him. I then asked Wendy to please step aside so I could hold him alone for the last time. She sat back down on the couch.

I cried so hard and long that my body seemed to convulse as if it were going into shock. Then suddenly I felt light and my mind seemed more alert for some reason. The vet asked if I'd like to keep some of his fur. Oh, yes please. She took a pair of electric grooming shears from her case, plugged it into the nearby wall socket and shaved some off his back. I then asked for some white fur from his front legs, which still looked like he was wearing a pair of white socks, and a bit of brown fur with a tinge of black from his side. She shaved off a few pieces from my requested areas, placed all of it in a Ziploc® bag, and put it aside.

She then explained the next shot would stop his heart. She took the cap off the syringe, and plunged the needle into the glass vial containing the liquid that would send my Snoopy to his final breath. I watched as the syringe sucked up the liquid, and I heard a popping sound of metal coming out of plastic as she pulled the needle out. She tapped it a few times and pushed the plunger in, forcing air out along with a few drops of the liquid. The shot was ready. She inserted the needle into Snoopy's right front leg. While she was doing this, she explained everything in detail, though I can't remember what she said. She gave Snoopy the shot. It didn't take long to stop his heart, a minute or two that seemed like hours. She listened with a stethoscope and nodded, he was gone.

So was I. I cried even harder. Tears, snot, and saliva poured from my face. I cried harder for my boy than I had over my parents passing, or anyone else I've known to die. I wiped my face and blew my nose with tissue. Wendy, too, was a wreck of tears.

Lying lifeless on our living room floor was my boy. I could not hug his dead body. I was more than freaked out, but I had to be strong and get done what needed to be done. The vet's business was over and she was ready to leave. I walked her to her truck, thanked her, and said goodbye.

The whole ordeal took less than ten minutes. The man from the pet cremation service was patiently waiting. I gave him a check for the fee we agreed on. He backed his white van into the driveway, exited, and opened the rear windowed door. There in the back was the spot he was to place Snoopy, and take him to the crematorium.

I walked him into the house. He saw Snoopy's lifeless body lying on his blanket. He'd probably seen hundreds, maybe thousands, of dead pets in his time. He asked me if I wanted to carry Snoopy out to the van. I said no. I could barely walk or talk. He picked Snoopy up and to my surprise his bodily fluids did not come out after he passed. The blanket and plastic sheet were completely dry. Even in death he was still a good boy, never ever peeing in the house. He held it in like he had his whole life, knowing it was the right thing to do.

The man carried him to the van and placed him in the back. Wendy and I cried, reached in, petted him and said goodbye for the last time. The man shut the windowed door. I thanked him and shook his hand. He got in the van, started the engine, and proceeded down our driveway. I watched it move along our street until it turned the corner and was out of sight. It would be ten days before I could pick up Snoopy's ashes.

Our house, on Cheerful Valley Avenue, was anything but cheerful.

-40-

AFTERWARDS AND BEYOND

With all the stress and worry regarding Snoopy, I didn't pay too much attention to Melvin. Snoopy was his best friend and now he would no longer be in his life. This most likely would have an effect on him, but you never know with cats, especially Melvin. Where was he when his best friend was being put down?

After Snoopy was taken away, Wendy and I searched the house for Melvin. He rarely ever came out when you called his name. We looked in his familiar hiding places; under the bed, in the upstairs bathroom cabinets, underneath the kitchen sink, even above the refrigerator atop the kitchen cabinet, in an area he once hid when he was scared by some workers in the house. We couldn't find him. Did he wig-out and slip out the front door when no one was looking?

After twenty minutes of searching, I finally found him in the master bedroom closet, hiding in a corner behind a suitcase. How he got in there, I never knew. He looked scared and upset. I picked him up, comforted him, and handed him to Wendy. Poor kitty. He knew something was wrong. He knew his buddy was gone. The sadness was in the air.

It was hard for me to function. My boy was such a huge part of my life; it would take time getting used to him not being around. I had to face the fact he was gone. It wasn't like I left him at a friend's house while I was away on a job, or on vacation. He wasn't coming back. He was physically gone forever. No more walks, playing, feeding him, seeing him smile, having his comforting presence near.

I can't compare my pain to the pain of losing a child, because I've never had a child. I never wanted to be a parent. I don't believe any human being should have that much power over another human being. There are too many people in the world who should never have conceived children and they unconsciously bring pain and havoc into the world. Snoopy was my child, and what a loving child he was.

I knew the day would come when he would no longer be in my life; I just wasn't prepared for it. I don't know how anyone can prepare for it. I read a few books regarding end-of-life issues for animals; how to cope afterwards, how to get through it. They were okay. Written by well-meaning people. I did a few writing exercises they suggested. I felt better not because of what the exercises asked of me, but because they took my mind off Snoopy. I even did a grieving journal for a while.

Maybe there are stages of grieving like some of the so-called experts claim. Maybe not. Who is anyone to tell you what stage or phase you're going through when the one you love, or the thing you love, dies? Whether it's an animal, a person, or even the loss of a favorite food you had to give up because it was destroying your health. My feelings are my feelings. If I want to cry, laugh, lash-out, hurt, not sleep, be depressed, be alone, for whatever period of time I choose—so be it. I didn't need anyone telling me *when* I'd get over something, or *when* I was supposed to *feel* something. How should they know? They didn't know me, or my life experiences. If I wanted to cry every day for a year, or two years, I would.

We were also in the middle of packing up our house. Our move back to Los Angeles was in two months. I was selling stuff I didn't need on Craigslist, and donating other stuff to the Las Vegas Rescue Mission.

A few days after Snoopy passed—even though I was numb, devastated, and depressed beyond words—I summoned up enough strength to send out a memorial email to friends and associates. Mostly to those who met Snoopy, or spent time with him. Along with the memorial I attached various photos of him taken over the years.

Many of the responses to my email were pretty standard: "I'm sorry for your loss," "My heart goes out to you," and so on. My few close friends, who knew Snoopy, wrote more elaborate and personal responses. My neighbors across the street, Don, Jackie, and her kids, Harlan and Skylar, were saddened by his passing. People react differently to death, whether it's over people they've known, pets, the death of a relationship, a job, or even the death of a public figure known only through the media.

I merely wanted people in my life to know Snoopy was gone. He had touched many of their lives, and it was only proper for them to know he was no longer with us.

-41-

PICKING UP THE ASHES

Wednesday, November 23, 2010. I called the pet crematorium around 8:30 AM, when they opened. They told me Snoopy's ashes were ready to be picked any time. It was ten days since he was gone. My focus was not good. I barely ate. I was still crying a lot, merely going through the motions of life. Missing him so much I wanted to die.

Wendy delved into her work to take her mind off Snoopy. I thought it best not to have two completely devastated pet owners—who could barely function—show up at the crematorium to get his ashes, so I asked my next-door neighbor, Linda, to drive me. She said okay and even canceled a previous appointment to accommodate me. I didn't feel emotionally stable enough to drive my car. I didn't know how I would react when I would be handed what was left of Snoopy in a box. I didn't know if I would break down crying. I felt I might be on the edge of a nervous breakdown.

The crematorium was in Henderson, Nevada, about a 20 mile drive. It was located in an industrial section of town in an inconspicuous building with a simple company sign located near the driveway entrance to let you know they were there. Linda parked her car in the adjoining parking lot. We got out and entered the facility.

I gave my name to the woman at the front desk and told her I was there to pick up my dog Snoopy's ashes. She was fortyish, well-dressed, and seemed kind and gentle, like many people that work in the death care industry. You'd have to be, working in a place like that.

Can you imagine if the person you picked up your pet's ashes from was unkempt and just downright rude? *"Sit your rump down and I'll be with you when I get good and ready. Don't forget to take a number and wait your turn. It's been a busy morning—lots of dogs, cats, birds, a bunch of horses, and a moose died last week. We've had the furnace going nonstop, day and night. Plus, the storage freezers went out last night and the smell out back is horrific—a real fricking nightmare. Now keep your pie hole shut, I need to concentrate. I'm on Facebook right now and I'm getting really good at FarmVille."* Boy, there would be some fists flying.

The woman looked up my information on the computer. She said she would get Snoopy and left the room through the door behind her. I was antsy. My mind was hyper-alert. I carried a few tissues in my hand. I wanted to be ready for any held-back tears that might sneak their way down my face.

Linda and I browsed around the waiting area for a few minutes, looking at the various urns and products they sold. I then sat down, trying to hold myself together. That didn't last more than a minute. I cried so hard, I began hyperventilating; breathing in and out very quickly. Then I started to rock back and forth in my seat like a victim of child abuse, who can't communicate verbally. Linda and a couple other customers in the waiting area noticed how I was behaving. No one said a word. After the rocking stopped and I calmed down, Linda brought over more tissues.

Several more minutes passed. The woman from the front desk came back in the room and softly called out, "Mr. Camen." I wiped my eyes and got up. She placed on her desk what looked like a cardboard takeout box. The box was about a foot long and ten inches wide. It was covered in black and white polka dots the size of silver dollars with a handle that opened and closed the top. She said the wood urn I ordered containing Snoopy's ashes was inside, along with a certificate of cremation, certifying the day he was cremated, and a receipt. I was glad it was packed away. If she would have handed me only his urn I would have lost it right then and there. They would have had to call an ambulance. I thanked the woman, and Linda and I left.

On the drive back home I held the box in my lap. I don't remember talking much. I just wanted to get the urn home and look at it in private. Linda dropped me off in front of my house. I thanked her, took the box inside and went up the stairs to second floor.

I walked down the hallway and sat on the carpet near my office door with the box in front of me. I looked at it for a moment; a long sigh came out of me. Every part of my body was stressed. I could feel the skin around my eyes had slightly swollen from crying. I took a deep breath then opened the box. The urn was inside a black velvet bag with a draw string. It looked similar to those used to package expensive whiskey bottles. I opened it and removed Snoopy's ashes. They were in a sealed wood box about eight inches long by six inches wide, and a few inches deep. On the front was an engraved brass plate with the simple words I requested, "Snoopy, My Best Friend Forever." On top was a small magnetic plate with an attachable four-by-six plastic picture frame for Snoopy's photo.

I got up, went into the master bedroom closet, searched through the photo albums and found one of my favorite Snoopy photos. It's a close-up of him smiling with his mouth slightly open. You can see the small round black birthmark on his tongue, about the size of a dime. He looks beautiful. I placed the photo in the picture frame and attached it to the urn. I had what was left of my boy. I found it quite strange. It was my first time dealing with cremation. It was mind-boggling to think the remains of all that love was in a small box. It creeped me out and fascinated me at the same time.

The urn now sits on a bookshelf next to me in my office. Along with it are Snoopy memorabilia from the Snoopy *Peanuts* character I've collected over the years. Not much, only a few pieces. I also framed the slip of paper from the Burbank Animal Shelter with Snoopy's intake information. It sits next to his urn symbolizing the start of my greatest friendship.

-42-

MISSING MY BOY AND CAR ACCIDENT NUMBER TWO

In the weeks following Snoopy's passing, I didn't feel much better. I was going through life on automatic pilot. I couldn't bear not being with him. Nothing else seemed to matter. I didn't want to live. I've never thought of myself as the most positive person in the world, or the most negative—I'm somewhere in-between. If you're aware of what's going on in the world, and what's going on around you, it's hard to see everything in a positive light. Snoopy had been the most positive light in my life, and he was gone. The most constant love I've ever known was gone and it was extremely hard to deal with.

I had been depressed and lonely before, but never like this. I thought of killing myself. I wasn't going to take one of the several guns around the house and blow my brains out, or slit my wrists. I'm too big of a baby for something so dramatic and messy.

I imagined a more peaceful death. A drug that would kill me in my sleep sounded more my style, if one could have a suicide style. You take a pill or a needle full of something and it's over. Goodnight forever. I didn't do any research on what kind of drug to take. My thoughts of suicide lasted a while, but they weren't strong enough for me to take action. I thought about what my death would do to Wendy. I also thought of Snoopy. He would never have wanted me to be hurt or hurt myself, let alone die. So, I let those suicidal thoughts move on down the highway. I would get through this like I had many other tough times in my life and come out a better person for having done so. There would be gold at the end of the rainbow.

However, the depressing thoughts and feelings created by his death kept coming, and they affected me in other ways. Driving my car took on a different meaning. It still had remnants of Snoopy's fur in the backseat and throughout. Though I had combed him out about once a week for most of his life, he still shed. I could still smell his smell and feel his energy, every time I got in the car. Memories would flow into my mind whenever I took a drive. It disturbed me. Was it safe for me to drive? I wasn't sure. I didn't know if it was safe for me to do much of anything with the wound of his death still young and all around me.

On December 6, 2010—23 days after Snoopy was gone—I got in a car accident. I was crossing a busy intersection on Blue Diamond Rd., about a half mile from my house. I was on my way to get an oil change at one of those "chain store tire places." I was doing *stuff* to get my mind off my pain and depression. As I crossed the road to make a left hand turn, it seems I didn't judge the distance of the cars speeding by in front of me. It was a few minutes before 9:00 AM. People were on their way to work. I pulled out and—BAM! I was hit in the driver's side door by a car going at least 55 miles-per-hour. The speed limit was 45.

My car spun around from the impact. Two more cars hit me and I spun around again. I was what they call in the car accident game, "T-boned." My car was totaled. It happened in seconds and I barely saw anything. I was told this is what happened from a police report. I was in a daze, my head was spinning. I was hit so hard *both* my car's airbags went off. My knees banged into each other, and my right knee slammed into the automatic stick shift, causing it to swell slightly. The powder from the airbags practically choked me. The insurance investigator later told me after observing my vehicle that he was shocked I didn't need to go to the hospital.

I got out of my car. My ears were ringing from the impact of the airbag to my face. The first thing I heard, as I was stumbling about, was the woman who ran her car into my driver's side door screaming at me for causing the accident. Her voice sounded muffled because of my ringing ears, but I could tell she was screaming because of her body language and the large movements of her mouth.

Glass, car parts, and all the junk from my car's trunk were scattered on the road. Tow trucks were called. I exchanged insurance information with the drivers involved. The police were called and a cop gave me a ticket for causing the accident, even though he didn't see what happened, and everyone who hit me was speeding. I was in no mood to argue with a Las Vegas police officer.

I called my neighbors, Linda and Tom. They happened to be home and were able to pick me up. They took me, and the junk from my car trunk, back to my house. In the days and weeks to come I would find out just how much I was hurt, since car accident injuries tend to show up late, like an arrogant rock star who has disdain for his fans. It wasn't too bad. My neck, back, and knees needed some chiropractic treatment. Thankfully, I had good insurance. I was covered.

I liked my car. I'd had it for five years, it was a great car. I bought another Camry as soon as I could.

I've always believed accidents happen for a reason. I couldn't bring myself to get rid of my car with the memories of Snoopy haunting me. The universe had other plans. With this car accident, I added more stress to my life. We were moving back to Los Angeles in about six weeks, and there was still plenty of packing and organizing to do.

-43-

BACK TO LOS ANGELES

It took Wendy and me about three months to pack up our house for the move back to Los Angeles. We did it a little bit at a time. Moving is stressful and a real pain, but the process of packing helped take my mind off the other stresses in my life. Boxes were stacked everywhere throughout the house and garage. I got real good at using a tape gun, but I don't think it's a skill I'll be adding to my resume anytime soon.

We moved on January 17th, 2011. Since we were going through the housing crisis at the time, we could have stayed in our home for several more months without paying the mortgage. I didn't want to. The sooner we got out of Las Vegas, the better.

One good thing about Las Vegas is that housing is now very cheap compared to many places in the country. A young couple starting out can buy a beautiful home in a good neighborhood and their mortgage can be less than paying rent. But you have to be able to stomach the heat. We merely had bad timing when it came to buying a house, like millions of others throughout the country.

Our move went fairly smooth. I hired the same movers who had moved us to Las Vegas four years and four months earlier. They got everything loaded into the truck and driven to Los Angeles in one day. Not bad, considering it was a 2100 square foot house with a two-car garage, and a four to five hour drive each way. They arrived at our new home in the early evening and unpacked the truck the following day. Wendy left early in the morning on the day of the move with Melvin to get him acclimated to *his* new home.

I was glad to be back in Los Angeles. The Los Angeles I had grown sick of now had new meaning. I felt invigorated, like I had when I had first come there as a teenager. The city hadn't changed—I had. Seems I needed a break for a few years.

Las Vegas had too much loss to deal with. We lost two houses. Work was lost because Las Vegas had very little for me; at least work I was used to. They only offered low-end jobs that were not worth my time, talent, or effort...and most of all, the loss of Snoopy.

Living in our Las Vegas house was not pleasant for me after he was gone. I couldn't get the image out of my head of him being euthanized in the living room. I couldn't sit on the couch, watch TV, or stay in the adjacent kitchen for more than a few minutes without seeing his lifeless body on the carpet. I had to walk over the spot where it happened to get to the kitchen. It got to the point where I'd make my meals in the kitchen and eat them upstairs in my office. Most of my time was spent upstairs.

I was glad to be back in Los Angeles, where I belonged. Also, Wendy's family was in Los Angeles and they were happy to have her back. Work seemed to pick up right away. Voiceover jobs came in and the money started to flow. No more driving back and forth from Las Vegas for work. I was back in the hub of the entertainment industry, and grateful to be in it.

EPILOGUE

There is no ending to the story of Snoopy and me. He is a continuing presence in my life. He is constantly with me in heart, mind, and spirit. No one can take him from me. I think about him all the time. I only wish my thoughts, which create my reality, could bring him back. Though I don't believe in any afterlife, I do believe in love. His love lives within me. I can't put it into words; it's a feeling, a feeling he gave me. I also believe in energy. Energy is all around us. I believe Snoopy's energy is with me sometimes. He's never left me. When I die I plan on having his ashes buried with me, or if I decide to be cremated, I will have his ashes mixed with mine. I have not yet made up my mind how I want my remains to be handled. I have too much living to do.

I've never been quite the same since the day he died. A part of me has ceased to exist. I still cry a lot, missing him, mostly in private. I can't be around dogs very long without crying. I can pet a dog for a little while, watch dogs as people walk them, but if I hang around them too long the memories of my special boy start to flow in and I become distraught. I know it's not a good thing.

Other aspects of him being gone from my life are sometimes difficult to deal with. For instance, I can't look too long at things I used to buy him. If I go into Trader Joe's, the specialty retail grocery store where I used to buy his doggie treats and glucosamine-chondroitin supplements, I can't look at the pet section too long without getting upset. If I look too long, tears will appear. I avoid that area of the store.

I don't like to spend time in a pet store shopping for Melvin. All the fun memories of Snoopy and me, shopping at PetSmart® and Petco®, come flowing into my mind and I become upset. Wendy shops for Melvin without me. I accept these reactions. It's the way it is for me right now.

I cry when I clean his urn. I wipe off the dust, kiss his picture on top, and weep. I don't walk around like an open wound all the time. It's only when I come into close contact with things related to him. I carry this with me and maybe my emotions will fade with time. Only time will tell.

When I'm in conversation with someone and they mention their dog or dogs, I show them his picture, which I keep as the main screensaver on my cell phone. Their reaction is usually the same; a compliment on his good looks, or his innate sweetness. My boy still wows them.

Snoopy was here for many reasons. To bring joy into both our lives, and to show me how to be a more loving and caring person, not just to him, but to others in this world. Before Snoopy, I had more of a hard edge to my personality. He helped change me for the better. Maybe in the way a person changes for the better when they become a parent to a child.

I may still be a bit cynical and sarcastic at times, but deep down I do want the best for people. I think he helped bring that out in me. He also taught me that our relationship was much more important and significant than the sometimes superficial world of Hollywood, where I spent so much of my time and energy.

I do cherish the time I had with him and the love I experienced. His time here was short, but "Oh, what a time we had." Some of the best, brightest, and insightful years of my life.

Though I am very opinionated about veterinary medicine, I am truly grateful for the two vets who helped Snoopy in the first several years of his life. Dr. Sheldon Altman, when Snoopy was a pup, and Dr. Carol Skaar, the last vet Snoopy went to before we moved to Las Vegas. Because of Dr. Skaar's great care and treatment we take Melvin to see her, when it's absolutely necessary.

If you've read this book, I sincerely hope you've enjoyed some of my stories and experiences, and possibly my points of view. Maybe you've been able to relate to some of the things I've gone through. Maybe I made you laugh. Maybe you'll go out and get your own special shelter dog. I've shared quite a bit of my personal life and feelings, and it's been very therapeutic for me. I needed to get it out...and I thank you for being here with me.

If you have the privilege of a dog friend—or friends—in your life, I don't need to tell you how lucky you are. You have a kind of love around you not available anywhere else.

Never treat a dog with anything less than love, and maybe one day, you and I will be able to do the same with all the humans we meet.

Just like a dog.

A POEM FOR SNOOPY

I took a break one afternoon while working on this book and went to a neighborhood park. I had a spiral notebook with an attached pen tucked under my arm. Memories of Snoopy were swirling in my head and the following is what came out. It's called...

213

I MISS...

I miss...your smile, the feel of your paw in my hand, your soft fur against my face, your sweet kisses, your fluffy wagging tail.

I miss...the excited sound you'd make when you knew you were going for a walk, the wolf-like howls you'd make when a fire engine siren was too near.

I miss...your warm presence illuminating my day, my nights, my life.

I miss...watching your nostrils dilate as you took in the smells when we'd walk past restaurants.

I miss...you lying near my feet, by the foot of my bed, and outside my office, protecting me from...whatever.

I miss...your unrelenting forgiveness, greeting me, and loving me as no one else could.

I miss...watching you run on grass in the park, sliding down the kiddie slide, and barking at those who you knew would do me harm.

I miss...our hikes in Griffith Park, massaging your neck, and watching you gobble down your dry food at every meal.

I miss...watching you lick almond butter from a spoon in my hand, licking the remainder from the roof of your mouth and then finishing it off with a bowl of water.

I miss...the smell of your wet fur after a bath, and then watching you sit up then jump up for a biscuit for being such a good boy.

I miss...watching you run up and down the stairs, and riding in my car with the wind gently moving the fur on your back.

I miss...watching you grow, and playing—at the dog park, in front of our house, with your cat friend, or wherever I took you. You were a happy boy, my boy, my love.

I miss...caring for you, loving you, being your best friend, being there for you when you fell ill; when you needed me most and when you didn't need me at all.

I miss...loving you like I've never loved another; you touching my heart and mind; leaving a mark on my being, making me a better person.

I miss...your gentle calmness, your unconditional love.

I miss...our time together.

I miss...being missed by you.

I miss...everything about you.

I miss...*you* and will miss you forever and ever...my dear, dear Snoopy.